MW00366856

WHAT PEOPLE ARE SAYING ABOUT SAM CHAND...

Sam Chand has dedicated his life to champion the success of others. Known as a "dream releaser," Sam is a leader of leaders who will constantly challenge and lift our mindsets, self-imposed limitations, and unexamined choices. Sam writes from the enormous wealth of his own experience with uncanny insight, good humor, and pragmatic advice.

—Brian Houston
Global Senior Pastor, Hillsong Church

Sam Chand's teaching is a secret weapon resulting in the increase of effective materialization of your unrealized potential.

—Bishop T. D. Jakes
New York Times Best-Selling Author

Sam Chand has been one of the most valuable mentors in my life and ministry. He has tremendous character, valuable leadership insight, a contagious sense of humor, and a pastor's heart. He has mentored me and made me a much stronger spiritual leader.

—Craig Groeschel
Senior Pastor, Life.Church

Samuel Chand is a leader's leader. His keen insights and vast leadership exposure have prepared him well for resourcing the kingdom. His natural passion for leadership development is a refined gift he enthusiastically shares with leaders and developing leaders.

—*John C. Maxwell*
Founder, EQUIP
New York Times Best-Selling Author

No one does this better than Sam Chand and I can say that from our experience working with him in my own church. His reputation for helping companies find their way in the twenty-first century is exemplary and his integrity is beyond reproach.

—*Jentezen Franklin*
Senior Pastor, Free Chapel
New York Times Best-Selling Author

Great leaders have mastered the art of asking great questions, but legendary leaders like Sam Chand have mastered the art of questioning their own thinking.

—*Steven Furtick*
Founder and Lead Pastor, Elevation Church

Change is on the horizon, but it will not come by accident—it will require intentionality by those who lead the way! As a voice of influence on the subject of leadership, my friend Sam Chand will help you shape your future by reshaping the way you think!

—*John Bevere*
Best-Selling Author and Minister
Cofounder, Messenger International

One of the most respected voices on church and ministry leadership today is Sam Chand. On his website, his tag line is, "My life's vision is helping others succeed"—and he's good at it. Sam and I have shared a number of clients over the years, and time and time again, I've seen him turn around struggling churches, inspire frustrated leaders, and transform the culture at failing organizations.

—*Phil Cooke*
Media Producer and Consultant
Author, *The Way Back*

Just when I thought my friend Sam Chand had reached his pinnacle, he transcends to a new dimension. Sam has a masterful skill of asking piercing questions, which are better questions that lead to better answers and ultimately a better life!

—*Bishop Dale C. Bronner*
Author/Founder, Word of Faith Family Worship Cathedral

Sam Chand will expand your thinking, give you fresh tools, and help you navigate your leadership journey.

—*Mark Batterson*
Lead Pastor, National Community Church

CH◀NGE
HAS
CH▶NGED

TIME FOR A STRATEGIC RESET

SAM CHAND

WHITAKER
HOUSE

All Scripture quotations are taken from *The Holy Bible, English Standard Version*, © 2016, 2001, 2000, 1995 by Crossway Bibles, a division of Good News Publishers. Used by permission. All rights reserved.

Boldface type in the Scripture quotations indicates the author's emphasis.

CHANGE HAS CHANGED
Time for a Strategic Reset

Samuel R. Chand Consulting
950 Eagle's Landing Parkway Suite 295
Stockbridge, GA 30281
www.samchand.com

ISBN: 978-1-64123-719-2
eBook ISBN: 978-1-64123-720-8

Printed in the United States of America
© 2021 by Samuel R. Chand
All rights reserved.

Whitaker House
1030 Hunt Valley Circle
New Kensington, PA 15068
www.whitakerhouse.com

Library of Congress Cataloging-in-Publication Data (Pending)

1 2 3 4 5 6 7 8 9 10 11 **WH** 28 27 26 25 24 23 22 21

CONTENTS

1

NEVER THE SAME AGAIN

We are all navigating this new normal together.
As we lock arms virtually and try to help one another
in the ways we can, our vast world suddenly feels a
little smaller and a lot more connected.
And for that, we are grateful.
—Michael Dell, CEO of Dell

Everyone is tired. Everyone is confused. Everyone is stressed. Since the spring of 2020, leaders in every organization and at every level have suffered from enormous stress. It's a fact that we minimize at our peril.

After several months of lockdowns, openings, more lockdowns, reopenings, and countless (often conflicting and confusing) updates about the virus, masks, and the promise of vaccines, I held a video conference with eighty-seven leaders of the largest churches in Europe. They were from all parts of the European Union. I assumed that their experience was similar to what I'd heard from leaders in the United States and around the world. Just a few minutes into our call, I said, "I know your heart is heavy, your brain is fried, you're exhausted, and you're frazzled by all the new and rapidly changing challenges during the pandemic."

Instantly, all of the heads in the little boxes on my computer screen nodded. In the environment of the call, I had given them permission to be honest about their mental stress and their physical exhaustion. They hadn't felt they could take off their mask of invincibility around the people on their teams, but they felt safe with me and each other.

As we talked, they had another insight: if they were that stressed and tired, the people on their teams felt even worse. As the primary leaders of their organizations, they had options. They could, at least to some degree, protect their bandwidth by saying "no" to some demands and requests, but the people on their teams had far less flexibility. They were under the gun to respond to the leader's immediate decisions about media, information technology, facilities, and programming—and for those who work in the business world, sales, production, research and development, and online marketing. On top of that, these team members were expected to get results even as the situation changed from day to day…and sometimes from hour to hour.

If the leader's stress level was at seven, the people on the team were at nine. The eighty-seven leaders on our call suddenly understood why everyone—people on their teams, their spouses and kids, and themselves—had hair-trigger reactions to seemingly insignificant events and walked around with a toxic mixture of anxiety, sadness, and resentment because things were changing so much and so fast all around them. After the call, a leader from Germany sent me this text:

> Thank you, Sam, for your exact and clear analysis of our current emotional situation. I felt so understood. And thank you even more for your helpful perspective. Actually, we're already doing a lot of what you recommend, but your input made it much clearer. I hope to see you soon in person, maybe one day in Germany! Many blessings.

Over and over again, I've heard leaders in business, the church, and nonprofits tell me, "Sam, I can't wait until all this is over and we can return to normal."

TOO MUCH HAS CHANGED FOR US TO GO BACK TO THE WAY THINGS USED TO BE. IN FACT, THE VERY NATURE OF CHANGE HAS CHANGED!

I completely understand this sentiment, but I gently and clearly inform them, "Yes, that would be wonderful, but I'm afraid it's not going to happen. Too much has changed for us to go back to the way things used to be. In fact, the very nature of change has changed! We'll be living with it from now on."

CLIMATE CHANGE

No, I'm not referring to fossil fuels, Western wildfires, hurricanes, and rising sea levels. I'm talking about our sociological ecosystem, which is experiencing far more stress in far less time than our climate. The first step in responding to a period of rapid change is to take a hard look at the change factors:

* We're experiencing the worst health crisis since the Spanish flu pandemic of 1918-1919.

In an article in *TIME* magazine, Laura Spinney compares the two health emergencies:

As the world grapples with a global health emergency that is COVID-19, many are drawing parallels with a pandemic of another infectious disease – influenza – that took the world by storm just over 100 years ago. We should hope against hope that this one isn't as bad, but the 1918 flu had momentous long-term consequences – not least for the way countries deliver healthcare.[1]

+ We're experiencing the biggest financial crisis since the Great Depression in the 1930s.

As the shutdowns took effect in the spring of 2020, many (if not most) businesses had to temporarily close or drastically change the way they do business. Online marketing and sales soared as people couldn't go to stores that were closed or chose to avoid contact in ones that remained open. As the seesaw of closings and openings continued, small businesses suffered. Kevin Kuhlman, the vice president of federal government relations for the National Federation of Independent Business, told *Fortune* magazine, "If the economic trend continues at this rate, one in five business owners anticipate they won't make it." More than 100,000 businesses have permanently closed, devastating the owners, employees, and their families.[2] This staggering number represents 60 percent of businesses that closed temporarily during the pandemic.

+ We're experiencing the greatest social upheaval since the 1960s.

Some readers may not be old enough to remember, but the Sixties saw civil rights marches; violence against the Freedom Riders who rode buses into the South to advocate for Black suffrage; Birmingham police chief Bull Connor turning fierce dogs and water cannons on peaceful protesters; the assassinations of President John F. Kennedy, his brother Robert, and Baptist minister and civil rights leader Martin Luther King Jr.; subsequent riots throughout the country after King's death; police violence at the Democratic National Convention; and the shooting of four unarmed students by National Guard troops at Kent State University. And all of this took place as the nation was bitterly divided over the unpopular Vietnam War.

In the summer of 2020, a number of cities saw peaceful protests against the killing of Black people turn violent. When governors and mayors appeared to be impotent to quell the violence night after night, many in the country were outraged. Instead of coming together to find justice, both sides hardened in their animosity toward each other. Many churches, especially those that have done a good job of reaching a diverse population, have seen lines drawn in their congregations. Far too often, the lack of empathy they see on the news has been replicated in their relationships with those in the church who have a different ethnicity, background, and socio-economic status.

Every news program is like a daily report about a hostage crisis. The reporters tell terrible news and give dire warnings. It didn't take long for many people to avoid broadcasts entirely, but they still face the continual weight of the problem. We all are suffering:

+ *Grief* over the loss of people we love, routines that made us feel comfortable, the feeling of safety, and closeness to our friends and family.

+ *Resentment* because those we've trusted have failed to protect us, failed to provide for us, and don't seem to have answers to the most pressing questions.

- *Anxiety* because uncertainty robs us of a solid foundation of trust and comfort.

- *Polarization*, which existed before the pandemic, but now divides us on everything from masks and vaccines to election results.

- *Financial strains*, especially in the lives of owners and employees whose businesses have closed and who have lost their jobs.

- *Suspicion of leaders* because a knee-jerk effect of stress is to question the intelligence and integrity of those who are making decisions.

- *Epistemological uncertainty about what is true* because nearly everyone on the Internet claims or appears to be the preeminent expert on every topic—and lashes out furiously if anyone dares to disagree.

- And we worry about how all of this is affecting *our children*, who miss interactions when schools are closed and absorb the "worry rays" we emit in the atmosphere of our homes.

Of course, the negative impacts of the pandemic don't affect us equally. Few of us endure all of these factors, but virtually all of us suffer from at least a few. Some people have seemingly flourished in this painful season. Investors have made a lot of money, but money can't buy security and love. And those who were on the margins of society, like many in our churches and who used to shop in our stores, are being hit with a sledgehammer of stress.

THOSE WHO WERE ON THE MARGINS OF SOCIETY, LIKE MANY IN OUR CHURCHES AND WHO USED TO SHOP IN OUR STORES, ARE BEING HIT WITH A SLEDGEHAMMER OF STRESS.

In a sobering personal reflection about life during the pandemic, *National Review* writer Michael Brendan Dougherty realized he and others had resorted to arms-length, clinical language to describe the emotional toll: "We feel we are allowed to speak of the 'mental-health effects' of lockdowns, closures, and the fear-driven lack of sociability on ourselves and our children. But when we do, we talk about ourselves like lab animals, as if we were neutral observers of our lives." But the year wasn't a total loss. Dougherty absorbed important lessons. "Personally, the last year has fortified my conviction that life cannot be lived via screens, and that the summer — when it comes — should be filled with big get-togethers...and many hot tears over what we've lost."[3]

NO QUICK RETURN

We often think of "the lingering impact of COVID" as a health concern, and indeed it is. Doctors have identified "long haulers" who continue to suffer adverse effects of the virus months after the initial infection. They also report alarming cases of the virus's permanent damage to organs, such as the liver, kidney, lungs, and heart.[4] There has also been competing and conflicting information about the safety of the COVID-19 vaccines themselves. But physical effects are only part of the painful legacy of the pandemic. A preliminary report on the impact of social distancing calls this a "double pandemic" and suggests the effects will be with us for a long time:

> With the exception of "essential workers," the pandemic has meant limiting physical proximity to those with whom one lives. For the 28 percent of Americans who live alone, this has meant little to no human contact for months. Regardless of living situation, interactions with anyone outside the home have been severely limited for everyone. Preliminary surveys suggest that within the first month of COVID-19, loneliness increased by 20 to 30 percent, and emotional distress tripled. While several surveys are still ongoing to capture the full extent of the problem, current evidence suggests the pre-existing public health crisis of social isolation and loneliness may be far more widespread than previously estimated....Proximity to others, particularly trusted others, signals safety. When we lack proximity to trusted others our brain and body may respond with a state of heightened alert. This can result in increases in blood pressure, stress hormones,

and inflammatory responses—which if experienced on an ongoing basis can put us at increased risk for a variety of chronic illnesses.[5]

CHANGE AGENTS

Leaders—the primary executives and all of those who lead throughout our organizations—are *change agents* who anticipate the need to make shifts and bold decisions. They are *change leaders* who help their people take steps forward. The problem, as I've pointed out, is that many of us are exhausted mentally, physically, emotionally, and spiritually, and those we lead are weighed down by uncertainty, grief, anxiety, polarization, and a nagging suspicion that their leaders (that's us) in every walk of life don't really know what's going on. Virtual meetings have saved businesses and jobs, but the lack of meaningful contact is like getting tiny sips of water every so often in a desert: we're staying alive, but we're still thirsty and unsatisfied. More than ever, our organizations and our people need us to give them three essential ingredients: clear direction, empathy, and a sense of hope. Without them, the effects of pandemic-induced stress will continue to erode vision, joy, and creativity. But with them, people can learn and grow from this difficult and extended season of uncertainty.

It's easy to feel overwhelmed by the avalanche of news, which is mostly bad news and warnings that *things will get even worse!* If we're not careful, we'll either become reactive without thinking—which causes our people to doubt our wisdom—or we'll become passive and sullen, which invites them to look somewhere else for direction. Even after we achieve herd immunity and businesses and churches reopen, the damage of the past year or so will stay with us. In the continuing uncertainty, leaders need to ask five crucial questions:

1. What should we *start?*

For some, it's inconceivable to make plans to start something new as they cope with tragedy and loss, but great leaders know that down times (in the market and the community) offer incredible opportunities to those who are wise and nimble.

2. What should we *stop?*

We realize that at least some of the meetings, programs, and events we planned in "normal" times don't fit any longer. We'll be wasting our time and resources if we insist on continuing them.

3. What should we *suspend* until later?

Some activities will be appropriate later, but not now. We need to triage our plans to focus on those that will make the biggest difference in the short term.

4. What needs to be *sustained* at all costs?

Organizational values cannot be sacrificed in any way. The *what*, *how*, and *when* may change, but the *purpose and values* remain the organization's guiding light.

5. What will accelerate our *speed* of growth?

In a sustained crisis, people in the community and potential customers are looking for organizations that can adapt to the changing environment, speak to their emotional needs as well as their physical needs, and offer services and products they desperately want. The churches and businesses that see these opportunities will grow...and the others will falter and perhaps die.

These are important questions when things are going well; they're crucial when we face times of uncertainty, strain, and doubt.

FLEXIBLE...AND QUICK

It's almost comical: every pastor I've talked with since the pandemic began has told me they'd had long-term plans to utilize their online platforms, but they were forced to implement them within days when a lockdown was announced. Suddenly, planning and implementation were compressed into a flash!

A crisis brings out the worst or the best in people—and sometimes the worst and the best in the same person! Some crater under the strain, but others become more creative, more affirming of those who contribute, more patient with those who are struggling, and more willing to take bold risks. Leaders who adjust their plans to support their employees earn enormous reservoirs of trust and respect. For instance, when a fast-food chain had to close with no foreseeable date to open again, management avoided layoffs by partnering with a health and wellness company that needed help with a spike in online orders.

In a crisis, careful, detailed, vetted planning is no longer an option. The risk isn't making a *bad* decision; it's making *no* decision. An article in *McKinsey Quarterly* observes that organizations that remain too bureaucratic, slow, and focused on profits more than people are falling behind. It explains:

> Inertia is clearly riskier than action right now, so companies are mobilizing to address the immediate threat in ways they may have struggled to when taking on more abstract challenges, such as digital technology, automation, and artificial intelligence (all of which still loom). Bold experiments and new ways of working are now everyone's business. Will the new mindsets become behaviors that stick? We don't know. Did it take a pandemic for organizations to focus on change that matters? Too soon to say. Still, as one leader we spoke with puts it, "How can we ever tell ourselves again that we can't be faster? We have proved that we can. We're not going back."[6]

In times like these, any factors that have masked the true nature of management are stripped away, and the true organizational identity is revealed. Pastors and business leaders have a golden opportunity to show that their values are more than lip service about integrity, compassion, and unity. Character is taken for granted or overlooked in the good times, but it's plainly evident when the chips are down and people are struggling. People look into their leader's eyes and listen for the tone of voice that says, "We'll get through this, and we'll do it together. You can count on me, and we can count on each other."

In times of uncertainty, minds wander, vision wanes, and action diminishes—unless leaders encourage their people to do something that makes a difference every day. It may not be huge, but showing compassion and taking definitive action to help someone gives employees a sense that they're having an impact—because they are.

A word that I've heard again and again in the pandemic is *pivot*. The organization was going in a certain direction, but the crisis forced the leaders to change course and to change on the spur of the moment. A company that owns and manages a chain of theaters suddenly went from showing blockbusters to locking their doors. But the CEO didn't give up. In two days, management retrained 1,000 employees to work in the burgeoning retail grocery business. Do you think the theater employees feel valued by their leaders? I'm sure their loyalty has never been higher.

The bureaucracies and systems that worked well enough in normal times must be adapted for extraordinary seasons. Large meetings with lots of research and slow decision-making doesn't work in crises. Companies and churches are forming smaller teams and giving them more authority to act. Will they make some decisions they regret? Of course, but they'll show their constituents they're actively involved in meeting needs. And some segments of the organization that were ancillary before the pandemic, such as IT, are now vitally important to enable leaders to connect with members and customers. In other words, the organizational chart is being completely revamped. (More on that later.)

AS ORGANIZATIONS BECOME MORE FLEXIBLE AND ADAPT MORE QUICKLY, LEADERS WILL BE ABLE TO IDENTIFY THEIR OUTSTANDING TEAM MEMBERS, THE ONES WHO RISE TO THE CHALLENGE WITH A BLEND OF CREATIVITY, TALENT, OPTIMISM, AND TENACITY.

As organizations become more flexible and adapt more quickly, leaders will be able to identify their outstanding team members, the ones who rise to the challenge with a blend of creativity, talent, optimism, and tenacity. These are the people who lead the way into the future, the ones who capture the moment and turn chaos into opportunities. A McKinsey &

Company regular article entitled "The Shortlist" advises leaders to become flexible and quick. The risk, the author asserts, is that when the worst of the crisis is past, leaders will be tempted to go back to "business as usual."

> Now, as the world feels its way toward recovery, the risk is that inertia will set in, along with a longing for a return to the operating style of earlier days. In our conversations with CEOs, we are struck by stories of how some young middle managers are defying the problems and frustrations of this difficult period. Only by advancing new cadres of adaptive, resilient leaders, as well as a middle bench fluent in technology that cuts across silos, will companies be able to work with the speed and impact necessary. Time for some battlefield promotions.[7]

Indeed. Battlefield promotions are given because people exhibit courage, skill, and exemplary leadership in the heat of the moment—exactly the qualities leaders are looking for in their people right now.

MY PROMISE

My friends who live along the Gulf and Atlantic coasts have lived through more than their fair share of hurricanes, and they tell me there's something they dread more than the howling winds and pounding rain, which always seem to hit at night. They're more bothered by the long cleanup operations to put their homes, businesses, and communities back together.

The pandemic is the hurricane, and we've only just begun the prolonged season of cleanup. When we're done, however, our organizations can be stronger than ever, and we can be better leaders than we've ever been.

As you dive into this book, I'm making three promises:

1. First, you'll find plenty of understanding and compassion. I understand how you feel, and I empathize with the challenges you face.

2. I'll provide plenty of insights about the complexity of your situation.

3. I'll offer principles and practices you can apply—right now, today—to make you a better leader at this time when everybody needs you more than ever.

The old assumptions about decision-making, personnel, and processes no longer apply. This book will give you concepts that fit with the reality of our dynamically changing world.

(Author's note: I'm making a very large assumption that by the time this book is released, the worst of the pandemic will be over. As you'll see in these chapters, I believe the effects will be with us for a long time.)

TAKEAWAYS

+ During and in the aftermath of the pandemic, leaders are fried—emotionally, physically, mentally, and spiritually.

+ To lead effectively, we need to ask (and answer) five crucial questions:

    » What should we *start*?

    » What should we *stop*?

    » What should we *suspend* until later?

    » What should we *sustain* at all costs?

    » What will accelerate our *speed* of growth?

+ Speed, flexibility, boldness, and encouragement are more important than ever because the way we process change has radically changed.

At the end of each chapter, you'll find some questions to stimulate further reflection and provide opportunities for rich discussions with your team. Don't hurry through these. They're not timed tests! Carefully consider how you can adapt so you're flexible and quick.

THINK ABOUT IT

1. How would you describe the personal, family, and organizational stresses you've felt since the pandemic began?

2. How has stress affected your relationship with your team and your constituents (your leadership team and church members or business customers)?

3. On a scale of zero (not at all) to ten (all day, every day), how well have you adapted your leadership to be flexible and quick? Explain your answer.

4. What do you hope to get out of this book?

THREE MASSIVE SHIFTS

Nothing in life is to be feared, it is only to be
understood. Now is the time to understand more,
so that we may fear less.
—Marie Curie,
physicist, chemist, and nuclear scientist

Before the pandemic, when someone wearing a mask came into our stores or church, we called the police. Then, if someone *wasn't* wearing a mask, we called the police! Today, we're focused on things that we never gave a thought to before. When we call a meeting, will it be in person or virtual? When we walk into a room, are masks required or scorned? When someone coughs or sneezes, were we exposed to the most virulent variant of the virus? When we go to the grocery store, will some guy who acts like he's never shopped before lean over us to get a can of beans, or will he respect social distancing?

Who would have imagined we'd have to think about things like this?

In the late summer of 2020, the country was in turmoil with protests over racial discrimination and rioting associated with it in a number of cities, businesses were closing at an alarming rate, and the election campaign season was in full swing. I consulted with a pastor who has built a large, ethnically diverse congregation that meets in several locations. This pastor told me, "Sam, no matter what statement I make about any topic that's making the news today, half of our people will agree with me, and the other half will believe I've lost my mind—and my soul." He described how people in his congregation had for years reached across racial and cultural barriers to love each other, but in the fever-hot conditions in the summer, animosity had obliterated goodwill and understanding. He asked me to speak to his church...and the schedule worked out for me to go the Sunday before the election in early November. (Thanks a lot, pastor!)

As I studied and prayed in my preparation, I reminded myself that he had invited me to be an asset, not a liability. He hoped God would use me to help heal the divisions, not cause deeper wounds. I wanted God to speak to me and then through me so the church would be a bit more unified by deeper understanding and greater compassion, and the pastor wouldn't need to clean up any mess I caused by my message. In a culturally diverse church, emotions about the presidential candidates ran high. I couldn't ignore the reality of the tension, but I hoped my words and my tone would bring hope to dissolve at least some of the fury—on both sides.

Early voting had been going on for weeks, but it had stopped that weekend. The polls on Election Day would open about forty-five hours after I spoke. I love this pastor and I love his people. I certainly didn't want to be tone deaf as I spoke to them.

This wasn't an arbitrary concern. I knew a pastor who was asked to take sides a few months earlier when his racially diverse congregation was inflamed by unrest in the country. He told me he had to choose between taking one side, taking the other side, or saying nothing and continuing in the series he had already started. He chose to continue the series and avoid detonating the emotional explosives, but even his careful avoidance created a spark. The next Sunday, more than 1,200 people left his church because they concluded he wasn't sufficiently loyal to their side.

His church isn't the only one that has suffered. I know pastors whose churches have permanently closed their doors because people couldn't find a way to build bridges of understanding and love.

With these horror stories on my mind, I was well aware that my message on that Sunday before the election could have a powerful effect, one way or the other. In my friend's church, people had very clearly taken sides and they were emotionally charged in defending their positions. I wasn't going to be able to argue them out of their beliefs, so I had to appeal to them on a higher level. They may dispute facts (and alternative facts) about the cultural and political situation, but my task was to present them with God's higher truth, and then trust His Spirit to give them receptive hearts.

What was different in my preparation? I have always taught the truth of God's Word. I've consistently pointed people to Jesus as the Savior and Redeemer. And I've called people to align their desires, attitudes, and choices with the eternal truth and the values of the kingdom of God. But this time, I was aware of far more intense emotions and a risk level that was far greater than normal. As I studied and prayed, I practiced *conscious mindfulness*, carefully weighing each point—and even each sentence—to build, heal, and restore.

It's very easy to make assumptions that our audience shares our beliefs, but as our culture becomes more diverse and divided, leaders need to go the extra mile to understand different points of view, and just as importantly, to demonstrate that we understand the people watching and listening to us. And we need to realize that some common phrases are heard very differently by segments of our audience. For instance, if we say we value the sanctity of human life, we'll appeal to the right, but the left will suspect we advocate intrusion into the private lives of women. Or if we claim that Jesus showed special care for the destitute, the marginalized, and the outcasts, the left may cheer but those on the right may wonder why we didn't insist on personal responsibility. The list of examples could go on for pages, but you get the idea.

Let me make two points: first, if our audience is *not* diverse, we're doing a poor job of reaching out beyond our cultural comfort zones. Jesus went out of His way to reach a Samaritan woman with a shady past, a Syrophoenician woman who challenged Him, and a wealthy tax collector who was considered a traitor to his people. (See John 4:7–30; Mark 7:24–30; and Luke 19:1–10, respectively.) Do our congregations and employees have a multicolored hue? And second, our task as communicators is to think on a higher plane, to identify principles and truths that apply to everyone. Or to put it another way, we should be equal opportunity offenders! If we communicate that we only care about the needs and concerns of one group and not any other, we've failed to love like Jesus. That's the challenge for leaders today.

IF WE COMMUNICATE THAT WE ONLY CARE ABOUT THE NEEDS AND CONCERNS OF ONE GROUP AND NOT ANY OTHER, WE'VE FAILED TO LOVE LIKE JESUS.

Everything has changed, including your environment, you, and the people you lead. These aren't minor alterations; they're massive shifts. Take a look…

SHIFT #1: YOUR ENVIRONMENT HAS CHANGED

Perhaps the most common and most visible of the shifts in our environment is the massive number of people who suddenly exited office buildings and began working from home. In an article in *Forbes*, Falon Fatemi explains:

> According to research from Gartner, nearly three quarters (74%) of CFOs expect to transition a number of previously on-premise employees to remote work setups permanently in the aftermath of Covid-19. This transition is primarily driven by a desire to cut commercial real estate costs....In the post-pandemic era, while some companies will make the decision to transition 100% of their workforce to remote work, chances are that most companies will opt for a hybrid approach, allowing select employees to work remotely, or allowing all employees to work remotely some of the time. In order to recruit top-notch talent, companies are going to need to think very carefully about what their remote work policy will look like. Who is able to work remotely? Is there an application process? What does this look like?[1]

To be sure, some changes are permanent, but others are temporary. Online shopping for the full range of consumer goods was already increasing before the pandemic, and it won't decline much, if at all, after it's over. But many of us are counting the days until we can stop ordering takeout and return to our favorite restaurants.

How can we stay relevant in a culture in the middle of rapid change? In an article in *Harvard Business Review,* Michael Jacobides and Martin Reeves recommend cultivating a different point of view to capture the moment:

> In the military, a technique for discovering what you don't know is to use the "eyes of the enemy." Military leaders ask themselves, What is the enemy paying attention to? and then shift their own attention accordingly to illuminate potential blind spots and alternative perspectives. The same can be applied to industry mavericks and competitors: Who is doing well? What market segments are your rivals focused on? What products or services are they launching? The same principle can be extended to customers: Which ones are exhibiting new behaviors? Which have stayed loyal? What new crisis-induced needs do customers have, and what are they paying attention to?…In your own organization, ask: Which workplace innovations are taking hold in leading firms? What new needs are employees responding to? What opportunities do they represent that could potentially be developed and rolled out more broadly?[2]

Many of us don't see other churches or even other businesses as "the enemy." We're all working together to build and expand God's kingdom and provide for people in our communities. In a spirit of unity and shared sacrifice, we can learn from each other, share our successes and failures, and encourage each other to excel.

SHIFT #2: YOU HAVE CHANGED

If you think the stresses associated with the pandemic haven't affected you, you're living in a dream world. No, most of us haven't cratered under the pressure, but we've learned to live with rampant uncertainty and a raft full of nagging fears: "Am I going to get sick?" "What if we have to close down…again?" "Will the money hold out until this is over?" "How is this affecting our children?" "I haven't seen my elderly mother in months. I know she's so lonely." "I'm not sure I can come up with the right answers, or even come up with them fast enough."

As leaders, we've always carried the burden of casting vision, crafting plans, and leading people to a better future, but when the future is cloudy and people are looking to us more than ever, the burden can feel unbearable.

Fear of real threats is a very normal and necessary reaction. When a car swerves in front of us, a surge of adrenaline kicks us into high alert, and we react to avoid a collision. The immediate surge is quickly followed by a return to equilibrium. But what happens when it's car after car after car? Chronic adrenaline arousal causes us to be *always on*, hyperalert, and in reactive mode. Our bodies and our souls weren't meant for this. In addition to living *on edge*, we may experience racing hearts, headaches, an inability to concentrate, and inordinate sweating. These physical symptoms are usually combined with a sense of impending disaster. Thanks to our obsession with social media, some experts have called our new online behavior "doomscrolling." We may feel helpless and hopeless, become numb, have exaggerated emotional reactions to news events, and generally feel impatient and irritable.

Some of us have only brief bouts of anxiety, but others feel they've fallen into a pit of anguish and they can't find a way out.

SHIFT #3: THE PEOPLE AROUND YOU HAVE CHANGED

Yes, you're a gifted and gracious leader, but it's a mistake to assume that you've protected your team, your family, and others you serve from the stress of the pandemic season. Mental health has always been a concern for leaders in business, the church, and nonprofits, but the pandemic has accelerated the problem.

Lucy McBride, a primary care physician in Washington, D.C., observes:

COVID-19 has basically poured lighter fluid on a preexisting fire. We already had diseases of despair at very high levels in terms of addiction, depression, trauma, anxiety, isolation, loneliness, and more. The pandemic has only heightened preexisting mental health challenges. And many people are being forced to reckon with their mental health for the first time.[3]

Everywhere we turn, our lives have been affected by the virus. When we isolate, we're doing what the experts advise, but we miss the social interaction that is the oil and fuel of meaningful life. When we venture out, we wonder if we're exposing others to the disease…or if they're infecting us with each breath. Uncertainty is a corrosive mindset and lifestyle. Dr. McBride notes, "Trauma is the reaction to feeling unsafe. We're wired for safety, and with an invisible, ubiquitous, and potentially lethal virus in circulation, we simply don't feel safe. As a result, people are struggling with fear, vulnerability, worry, depression, and often adopt behaviors to numb those uncomfortable feelings."[4]

WHEN WE ISOLATE, WE'RE DOING WHAT THE EXPERTS ADVISE, BUT WE MISS THE SOCIAL INTERACTION THAT IS THE OIL AND FUEL OF MEANINGFUL LIFE.

In the early months of the pandemic, relatively few people actually knew anyone who had contracted the disease, but at the time of this writing, more than three in four people know someone who has been diagnosed with the disease. According to the World Health Organization, as of July 14, 2021, more than 187 million people have had the virus and four million have died from it. These aren't just numbers. Each one represents a deep well of worry, fear, and grief—emotions that are entirely normal, but when they become chronic conditions, they erode our ability to cope with difficulties. The irony is that when people need help the most, they often feel so over-whelmed that they don't have the energy to find a physician or counselor. People in remote or poor communities are especially limited in their ability to find mental health resources.

AN INFLECTION POINT

Crises create chaos, but they also offer opportunities for leaders to be creative and compassionate. The pandemic is an inflection point: the way things were isn't the way things will be. The healthcare system has been strained, and those who work in this sector are utterly exhausted, but we've learned to appreciate them more than ever.

After the devastating Spanish flu pandemic a century ago, city officials were motivated to build water and sewer systems, and healthcare services multiplied. After the terrorist attacks of September 11, 2001, thousands of people felt compelled to enlist in the armed services to protect our country. Today, the COVID-19 pandemic may inspire many to become health-care workers and enlist in other frontline careers because they want to follow the example of those who are currently serving. At every level of government, business, and the church, leaders are scrambling to figure out how to meet desperate needs and establish new systems that will last long into the future.

Rita McGrath is the author of *Seeing Around Corners*, which uses a visionary framework to anticipate change in the future. In an article about the pandemic, she imagines two plausible scenarios. In the first, leaders in government and business return to "business as usual" as quickly as possible and learn no lessons from the financial and cultural upheaval we've endured. If that happens, economic insecurity will increase for the people on the bottom half of the income spectrum, poverty will skyrocket, and political instability will increase. Social structures, like the church, nonprofits, and government programs for the poor, will be stretched to the breaking point, and unrest will accelerate.

A second scenario assumes leaders will pay attention to the root causes of inequity and realize the pandemic only accentuated an existing problem. But in this case, McGrath envisions leaders having the insight and courage to make bold changes, to care more about people than profits, and to launch initiatives throughout society to raise the standard of living for the marginalized. She suggests there is already some movement toward the second, more optimistic scenario, but fierce opposition exists. Business executives, politicians and other government officials, and church leaders have a choice: to stick their heads in the sand and hope things return to normal...or seize the moment, transform structures, and lead their organizations to a much better future. She concludes, "While these are not predictions about what is likely to happen (the world is too uncertain to predict with any confidence), it's clear that we are in the midst of some kind of inflection point. We're going to be asking questions about many of our taken-for-granted assumptions."[5]

No matter where and who you lead, you're in the middle of a society-changing inflection point. The pandemic has exposed problems that had been there all along, but now are far more evident. To use a geographic analogy, most of us have assumed that change was like the gradual erosion of a riverbank, taking a long time to reroute the channel. But this isn't like that. It's more like two tectonic plates that have been grinding against each other for a long time, building up pressure, and the pandemic released an earthquake that has shaken our previous assumptions. A friend who was in Pasadena, California, the night of the 6.7-magnitude Northridge earthquake on January 17, 1994, told me the shaking was terrifying and the aftershocks were unnerving, but it took months for people in the zone to adjust to the "next normal."

NO MATTER WHERE AND WHO YOU LEAD, YOU'RE IN THE MIDDLE OF A SOCIETY-CHANGING INFLECTION POINT.

The three massive shifts we've experienced are like three simultaneous earthquakes. Will we rise to the challenge and learn new ways to lead and love those who have been shaken?

In the rest of the book, we'll examine seven important organizational factors that are affected by the ways change has changed, including pace, people, process, programs, proclamation, preparation, and personal care.

TAKEAWAYS

+ Your ecosystem has changed, you have changed, and the people you lead have changed.

+ We need to learn how to practice "conscious mindfulness" so we can tailor our communication for each moment.

+ We're at an inflection point, and each of us has to decide if we're going to go back to the way things used to be or use the disruption to make bold changes.

THINK ABOUT IT

1. What are some ways the pandemic and its aftermath have changed your environment? How have you responded to these changes? What do you wish you had done? What have you done that will have a lasting, positive impact? What do you need to do right now?

2. Take a look in the mirror. How did the pandemic change your thoughts, attitudes, mood, and expectations? How many of those changes became entrenched and normal for you?

3. How has this difficult season affected your spouse, your children, your extended family, your team, and others you lead?

4. What difference does it make (or will it make) to practice "conscious mindfulness" as you adjust how you communicate with your family, your team, and your organization?

5. Of the two scenarios of the future, what needs to happen in you and through you to use the inflection point to initiate bold initiatives?

3

THE PACE OF CHANGE

In a crisis, don't hide behind anything or anybody.
They're going to find you anyway.
—Bear Bryant,
former University of Alabama football coach

The leader of a large organization called to ask for my advice. He explained that he was facing a major decision that would have a dramatic impact, and he needed to make it fast. After he explained the various options, I asked him, "Tell me, what are the protocols you normally use to make substantive changes like this?"

I heard a deep sigh over the phone, and then he responded, "Sam, we don't make decisions like this until we've thoroughly vetted the different choices. We have leadership meetings and focus groups. I consult with experts like you. We read books and articles, and we try to narrow down the options. When we land on two or three, we tease them out to envision the impact—positive and negative—of each one. We produce a pro forma for our investment of leadership, finances, space, personnel, and other resources. I work hard to form a consensus among all the top decision makers, listening to each one so they feel heard. After all of that, I make the decision."

I asked, "How would you define the essential elements of this whole process?"

He thought about it for a few seconds, and then he outlined five primary components of his usual process of decision-making.

I then asked the nuclear question: "When do you need to make this decision?"

I could almost hear him swallow hard. "By the end of today."

"Very good," I responded. "How many of the five can you fit into your timeline to make the decision by the end of the workday today?"

After a few seconds for him to do some quick analysis, he said, "Two."

"Okay." I tried to reassure him by sounding optimistic. "Use those and make the best decision you can. You can't do any more than that."

I'm not sure that's what he wanted to hear, but he seemed a bit more confident when we ended our call. Conversations like this have been repeated hundreds of thousands, if not millions, of times in organizations during the pandemic. Decisions that would have taken months of careful analysis and consensus building were compressed into hours...and sometimes minutes. Previously, leaders had the luxury of piloting organizational battleships or cruise ships, and they could take a long time to make a turn. Suddenly, they found themselves in a speedboat!

Shutdowns forced leaders of businesses, schools, and churches to make very quick decisions. Businesses had to quickly analyze if they could market and sell products online and how many employees they could keep. They had no idea if the change would last a few days or a year, but they had to consider the long-term implications of every snap decision.

Churches that had previously toyed with online services had only days to put all the pieces together, ramp up their production schedule, make sure their service provider had enough bandwidth, and communicate with their congregations that they could worship online the following Sunday. Pastors had to determine who could work from home and who, if anybody, needed to come to the office. They had to make decisions on the fly how to have funerals, weddings, and baptisms; how to administer pastoral care and counsel those who are struggling; and how to encourage people to keep giving when they didn't come to services.

Then, when the restrictions were lifted, the same whirlwind of decisions were made in reverse—with the mind-numbing realization that everything could be temporary until the next surge. In addition, many organizations had to make more drastic decisions to lock down because an outbreak among the staff required a ten- or fourteen-day quarantine.

VERY FEW ORGANIZATIONS HAVE ESCAPED THE DEMAND FOR RAPID CHANGE.

OUT OF CHARACTER

Very few organizations have escaped the demand for rapid change. I used to be the president of a university, and I've talked to people who are currently in similar roles about their challenges. As soon as the lockdowns occurred, they were forced to go to online classes. Their libraries were closed, so students tried to find enough online resources for their coursework. Virtually every college and university has some form of online programs, but professors who had been holding in-person classes had little to no training in online teaching. Before the pandemic, one in five of their professors taught online classes; suddenly, all of them did. Predictably, a few adapted very well, but many felt confused by the technology and the strangeness of looking at students in little boxes on the screen. They didn't grasp how the software works, they had no concept of how lighting affected their presentation, and they had difficulty converting handouts to PDF format so they could send notes to their students. This kind of rapid change is completely out of character for academic institutions.

When I led the university, if I'd wanted to make a major change to online classes, I'd first have my IT staff conduct a study and present me with their recommendations. I'd fine-tune their suggestions based on my analysis of our faculty and their courses, and then I'd present the ideas to them. If you know anything about professors and university administrators, you know they're not exactly wild and crazy risk-takers! They would want to launch study after study and then debate the findings ad nauseam. Even then, they would be very reluctant to make any decision that would shake things up too much. If, in fact, we came to the conclusion that we should move forward, each professor would need to submit a syllabus of their courses. When we had all of these, I'd contact our state's regulatory agencies and accrediting bodies for approval. I would need to coordinate with agencies that provide grants and loans for students to be sure the funding covered online courses, and I'd contact the Department of Homeland Security to be sure visas for international students wouldn't be adversely affected by the change to online classes. All of this would take at least a year and probably longer—and if it all worked out, we had some hard questions to answer: What would we charge our students? Would we need to charge less because they didn't come to the campus? If we charged less, did the budget numbers work for the school? And if we didn't charge less, how many students would drop out?

Of course, there are dozens of other crucial questions and important steps, but these give you an idea of the normal pace of change in an academic institution. When university presidents received the call that all academic institutions were being shut down, a year's worth of careful process was condensed into a few days. They didn't have time to fly board members in for consultation, and they didn't have time to meet with donors, key alumni, the faculty senate, or leaders of the student government to be sure they were on board with the new direction.

To make things even more complicated, universities have contracts with each member of the faculty. If professors don't want to teach online classes, termination may result in lawsuits.

RIGHT NOW!

Every leader has a story to tell. For instance:

+ A healthcare company that relied on major conferences to connect with new and existing clients had to find another way to stay relevant. With a single announcement from the Centers for Disease Control and Prevention (CDC), their business model was obliterated. In response, they crafted a new strategy in only two days, creating a service that identified COVID outbreaks to inform doctors and other healthcare providers and implementing it immediately.

+ A business that organizes garages, closets, and kitchens suddenly couldn't go to anyone's residence. They quickly crafted a virtual organizing service with a friendly employee to walk customers through the process of getting rid of clutter and solving the problem of messes at home.

+ A theater production company that worked with public schools was suddenly locked out of opportunities to be on-site with teachers and young actors. The company immediately came up with a new business plan to have online classes for the teachers and show them how to teach theater to their online students.

+ A bakery that had only dabbled in delivery services quickly expanded their website and hired more people to deliver goods. In fact, their delivery service proved to be so successful that they partnered with other companies to deliver their products, too, but instead of using this as an additional income stream, they offered this service at no charge to other business owners.

+ A clothing manufacturer completely revamped their operations when they heard reports that healthcare professionals were working without personal protective equipment such as masks and gowns. They quickly changed direction to produce two million washable face masks per week.[1]

+ Restaurants quickly shifted to takeout orders so they could stay in business and retain their employees.

+ Physicians were in a strange predicament. As infections increased, they wanted to keep contagious people out of their offices, but they still needed to see their patients. Some had previously tried telemedicine, but overnight, doctors throughout the country had to adapt to the new way of serving people. On a call, an individual can take his temperature and give his weight to the doctor, but few people have blood pressure monitors, heart monitors, or ways to gauge blood oxygen levels. Still, doctors found ways to provide quality care in a demanding environment by quickly learning to ask more specific, detailed questions so they could diagnose and treat people when they couldn't use a stethoscope, tongue depressor, or heart monitor.

For every company, church, and nonprofit, speed was essential. In the blink of an eye, careful analysis, vetting options, gathering input, and getting leaders to agree on the course of action became a luxury they could no longer afford. The pace of change had accelerated to lightning speed! These leaders have shown they have no limits on their creativity during a crisis.

ON STRINGS

Leaders have been like puppets dancing on strings as they react to national, state, and local requirements, which may be conflicting and are almost certainly temporary. At the height of the pandemic, we needed spreadsheets to determine if our organization could be open, what percent of occupancy we could have, whether masks were mandatory or optional, and how to respond to localized outbreaks with quarantines. National and statewide surges brought advisories from governors and mayors, forcing leaders of organizations to dance every time a string was pulled...which could be every day! And one thing is certain: every decision a leader made was accepted by some and fiercely resisted by others.

AND ONE THING IS CERTAIN: EVERY DECISION A LEADER MADE WAS ACCEPTED BY SOME AND FIERCELY RESISTED BY OTHERS.

The reactions of people in the organizations are more strings on leaders. It's easy to get caught up in trying to appease some at the risk of offending others. And if we move to soothe the feelings of those who are offended, those who were at first happy with us feel betrayed and become adversaries.

The public messages have been decidedly mixed: in the United States, the CDC issues guidance, but individual states have authority over the public health of their citizens. Some states had mandatory lockdowns while their citizens saw reports of people in other states going to restaurants and bars. It didn't seem fair! Governors tried to enforce stay-at-home orders while some federal officials encouraged people to get out, go to work, and enjoy their lives. Courts got involved, sometimes overturning a governor's orders. Exhausted healthcare workers pleaded with people to use protective measures to slow the spread of the virus, but plenty of blogs and posts claimed the virus is no worse than the seasonal flu.

In a classic case of confusion, as the disease numbers surged in the fall of 2020, New York City tried to slow the spread, but efforts by Mayor Bill de Blasio and Gov. Andrew Cuomo led to "chaos, confusion and tension" as emotions "erupted over restrictions that are closing schools and businesses and greatly limiting attendance at places of worship." The two leaders issued "competing hot-spot maps" that showed different levels of restrictions, but "schools and businesses that were to be shut down on one map were not on the other." Jewish and Catholic organizations filed lawsuits to stop the restrictions on worship.[2] It's no wonder that leaders and people in every sector of the city turned their anger on the governor and the mayor. That's what happens when quick decisions aren't communicated clearly.

MORE THAN EVER, LEADERS HAVE TO THINK AND ACT ON THE FLY TO COMMUNICATE WITH CLARITY, CONFIDENCE, AND KINDNESS TO EVERY PERSON ASSOCIATED WITH THE ORGANIZATION.

More than ever, leaders have to think and act on the fly to communicate with clarity, confidence, and kindness to every person associated with the organization. The urgency of decision-making may decline on the backside of the pandemic, but the lessons we learned during the crisis will help us make good decisions quicker in the future. That's what people expect from us, and expectation is reality.

TAKEAWAYS

+ In a crisis, leaders need to be pilots of speedboats, not battleships.

+ It's better to make a fast decision that has some gaps than to avoid making any decision at all.

+ Speed needs to be combined with optimism and creativity.

THINK ABOUT IT

1. Before the pandemic, what were the protocols you and your organization used to make important decisions? Think of one. How long did it take? Did you move quickly or hesitate?

2. During the pandemic, how did the pace of decision-making change for you? Describe one you had to make swiftly.

3. Some leaders are very intuitive. They make decisions as much on "feel" as on data. But others value detailed input and don't feel comfortable making decisions in haste. Which are you? Which would your team say you are? Explain your answer.

4. What lessons did you learn then that you're continuing to apply now?

4

PEOPLE OF CHANGE

We are, or will be, going through the most radical
transformation the world has ever seen;
people are justly terrified, excited, depressed,
heartbroken and hopeful, all at once.
—Heather Marsh, author of *Binding Chaos*

Before the pandemic, organizational decision makers consisted of six to ten top level people: the CEO, president or lead pastor, as well as the vice presidents or the executive team. Those who worked in IT, marketing, audiovisual, and customer service were far down the organizational chart. Decisions were hammered out in the C-suite, and everyone else was told what to do to hit benchmarks and achieve corporate goals. As the instructions were passed down the chain of command, good leaders asked for feedback and adjusted the plans, but the chain of command didn't change.

That was yesterday. Today is different.

A CEO told me that when the first surge hit and lockdowns occurred, he immediately realized he needed people with very different skills. The people on his executive team became obsolete because, as we saw earlier, the plodding process of analysis went out the window in a hurry. But something else happened that was just as dramatic and surprising: people who had been serving in obscurity suddenly became absolutely essential. He no longer needed the skillsets of the top managers, but he desperately needed people who could instantly change the business plan and implement a new strategy. The IT guy with long hair and jeans with holes in them could solve the problem of communicating with people who could no longer walk through the doors of the business. The lady whose name no one on the executive team knew because she was behind the camera in the marketing department became indispensable to get the leader's face and voice to people who were confused and needed direction. The most important room in the organization was no longer the executive suite, but the other part of the building where creative people worked their magic.

The executive team didn't have answers to the pressing, immediate problems, but the IT staff did. They had been dreaming of trying new things, upgrading their network, using different platforms, and making a bigger splash—and this was what they'd been waiting for! It wasn't much of a stretch for them to gear up, accelerate the development of systems, and tap into the expertise of a team that had been overlooked and underutilized.

THE URGENCY OF CHANGE IN THE PANDEMIC FLIPPED THE ORGANIZATIONAL CHART UPSIDE DOWN.

For this leader and countless others, the urgency of change in the pandemic flipped the organizational chart upside down. The leader's team looked very different; he needed the competence of a new set of people. The names on the doors and the slots in the formal organizational chart may not have changed, but the go-to people were different, and the leader's first stop every morning was down the hall to the IT offices.

This CEO didn't care what the organizational chart looked like; he just needed to get the job done, done right, and done right now! When one of the people on his executive team grumbled, the CEO let him know that the earth had shifted under their feet, and he'd better get used to it.

In a Ryerson University white paper on managing change, the authors insist that selecting a new leadership team is one of the most important tasks for a CEO, president, or pastor: "It is important to get the right people in place who are fully committed to the change initiative, well-respected within the organization, and have power and influence to drive the change effort at their levels."[1]

Obviously, some of the members of the previous team may disqualify themselves by their resistance or lack of sufficient enthusiasm for the new vision. In addition, their talents may not fit well with new strategies and technologies. Leaders who aren't willing to make hard decisions about the construction of the new team and try to give everyone—old and new members—equal authority run the risk of creating an unwieldy, complex, and fragmented leadership team...and that never works out well!

I often tell leaders, "Keep your eyes open to notice the people who are bringing you effective solutions to your real problems. They're the ones who will carry your organization into the future. Don't look at the job title on their HR forms. That may have been important before, but not any longer. Instead, look for people who are creative, optimistic, and effective, and pour your time into listening to them."

A CRISIS DOESN'T CREATE CHARACTER AND TALENT, BUT IT REVEALS WHAT'S ALWAYS BEEN THERE.

THE VENEER

A crisis doesn't create character and talent, but it reveals what's always been there. When the veneer of normalcy is stripped away, we see what people are really made of. Sometimes, they're exactly what we believed them to be, but we're often surprised. People who talked a good game may wilt under pressure, and those we may have overlooked might become warriors for our cause.

I encourage leaders to take notes about the people who perform in exemplary ways when the chips are down during a crisis so two things can happen: the leader can reward them and place them in roles where they can continue to contribute their knowledge and unique expertise after the pressure has lessened.

Actually, relating to these people may require a different approach from us. If we've been visionary, extroverted leaders, our style probably worked well in normal times, but during crises, we need to shift into a different mode. Instead of commanding first and listening second (if at all), the ability to tap into the skills of people who aren't normally on your team requires the talent of asking great questions, listening carefully, and asking follow-up questions to get more engagement and details. In an article in *Fast Company*, Krister Ungerböck explains:

> In crises, many leaders listen less because they believe immediate action is required. Usually, they are acting

from a mindset that using techniques associated extroversion is the only way to get ahead. Unfortunately, those leaders often forget that employees, the people actually taking the action, are key to navigating challenges.…When I adopted a "questions first" philosophy, my leadership abilities immediately evolved. I used to spend a lot of time coming up with solutions by myself before meetings, but leading with questions took less effort than leading with answers. I spent less time preparing and more time responding. The technique shifted the responsibility away from me, which helped position me as more of a listener and left me feeling less depleted. Posing questions helps others collectively solve problems. When people brainstorm their issues, they're more likely to take action without coercion or reminders.[2]

It may seem counterintuitive to listen more in a time of crisis, but the point is to listen to the right people, those who have the ability to solve urgent problems that seem to have come out of nowhere.

BEHIND THE SCENES

The other side of the equation is that in times of crisis, previous cracks in relationships often become gaping holes. One report showed that divorces were down during the pandemic, but not because couples were more loving and forgiving.

Instead, the courts were closed or backed up with cases. When the pandemic is over, experts expect a wave of divorces.

When many restaurants, businesses, and schools closed, millions of workers were furloughed, fired, or told to work from home. Domestic abuse hotlines prepared for an increase in demand because spouses and children didn't have the safety of their violent family member being away at work most of the day. However, they were surprised when the volume of calls actually declined. The reason, experts concluded, was that the victims couldn't safely connect with the services.

Economic disruption also contributes to spouse abuse. In an article entitled "A Pandemic within a Pandemic," *The New England Journal of Medicine* reports:

> Economic independence is a critical factor in violence prevention. For many people who experience [intimate partner violence], the financial entanglement with an abusive partner is too convoluted to sever without an alternative source of economic support. The pandemic has exacerbated financial entanglement by causing increased job loss and unemployment, particularly among women of color, immigrants, and workers without a college education.[3]

The same factors account for an increase in child abuse and maltreatment. Sometimes, emotional pain is unavoidable as families suffer sickness and death, financial hardship from the loss of employment, and the preoccupation of parents who are trying to make ends meet. But too often, the harm is the result of parents who are stressed beyond their limits—and the stress is multidimensional. It includes poor impulse control in parenting, marital conflict, increased substance abuse, financial strains from being out of work, and a general rise in tension that is the product of some or all of these factors. During this time, social isolation reduces the availability of valuable resources, so child abuse and neglect go unreported and unaddressed.

The *BC Medical Journal* reports:

> There has been widespread disruption of the communities and services that typically support children and families during times of stress. Physical and social distancing foster isolation and disrupt routines, and may limit access to extended family and other community support networks. Social workers, along with other health professionals, have been advised to minimize nonessential services that involve direct contact with families.[4]

In a desire to escape the stress, more people are turning to substances to give them relief. A survey of 1,000 adults showed an alarming 55 percent increase in alcohol consumption during the pandemic and a 36 percent rise in illicit drug use. These people identified their motivation primarily as attempts to reduce stress (53 percent), relieve boredom (39 percent), and cope with an existing mental illness, primarily anxiety and depression (32 percent). A psychiatrist for Baptist Health South Florida, Rachel V. F. Rohaidy, observes: "Our numbers are increasing—new patients with issues with alcohol use and established patients with a resurgence of their alcohol use."[5]

The closing of schools and the move to online learning may work well in adult education, judging by the many online degrees offered for those who are working and seeking a degree. However, children aren't faring as well.

WE MAY THINK OF SOCIAL ISOLATION AS AN EQUAL OPPORTUNITY PAIN, BUT IT'S MORE ACUTE IN SOME POPULATIONS.

A RAND Corporation survey found that two-thirds of teachers report that more than half of their students are falling behind academically; 56 percent of teachers say they only cover half or less than half of the curriculum they taught in-person; and students from disadvantaged communities have less access to computers and the Internet, plus they're missing free or reduced-price lunches, so hunger is a distraction as they try to learn. All of this puts enormous stress on teachers. They have to teach in an environment that's strange to them and their students, and the prospect of going back to in-person classrooms raises concerns over their health. Fully 84 percent said they have major or moderate worries about catching the virus and taking it home to their own families.[6] When schools open and "return to normal," teachers will find out how far students have fallen behind. The lag in progress will probably be evident in the lives of students for several years.

Over the past months, I've heard many people express heartache that they can't spend time with family members, especially elderly parents and grandchildren. We may think of social isolation as an equal opportunity pain, but it's more acute in some populations. A friend of mine has been communicating with a death row inmate for several years. The prison population is in close quarters with very little possibility of creating adequate distance to limit the risk of infection. My friend received a letter from the inmate describing months of lockdowns and quarantines of those who tested positive. The inmate wrote:

> There has been so much negative going on around here. There's been several suicides, guys hurting their cell mates, stuff like that. Everyone seems to be at their breaking point with having to be stuck in the cell for so long and not being able to call their family or take a shower and eating sack meals. It's really hard on everybody, and it's only bringing chaos. And it seems the world outside these walls is going crazy!

We feel called to care for the vulnerable—widows, orphans, the elderly, the poor, the hungry, the naked, and prisoners—but our compassion hits barriers that keep us apart.

Isolation weighs on all of us, and the absence or reduction of social contact leaves a hole in our sense of wellbeing. From time to time—and maybe a lot of the time—we're on edge, irritable, wary, and listless. Conflicting messages in the news and on social media arouse our suspicion, fear, and anger, so we gravitate to anyone who claims to have a definitive answer... about anything!

It's interesting that two of the articles I read about this phenomenon were entitled "The Pandemic within the Pandemic." The authors of these two articles, and many other experts who had different titles for their research and reports, predict that the relational disruption that is mostly hidden during the lockdowns will come to light as the virus gets under control. In other words, we're just beginning to see the damage that has been done since the first reports of a new virus out of China. Wise leaders anticipate these problems so they're not surprised, and the really bright leaders consider ways to help their people when the veil of isolation is removed and the problems become more evident.

IT'S ALL IN THE SYNAPSES

It doesn't take a psychologist to realize that the reactions we've seen during the pandemic fall into predictable categories: some are angry, defiant, and resistant; others try to escape their stress by self-medicating; and still others feel completely overwhelmed and crater under the heavy load of confusion and heartache. We can identify the obvious factors that create reactions to fight, flee, and freeze, but on a more fundamental level, our brains are hardwired to react these ways. Charles Stone observes:

> Our brain is wired to pick up threats and negative possibilities around us more than the positive. Two-thirds of the brain cells in the flight-fight part of our brain, the amygdala, are wired to pick up on the negative. Most people's initial response to change comes from these emotional centers rather than from their thinking centers.[7]

We want to reason with people, but when their brains are on high alert, their emotions dictate their responses. Since the dawn of humanity, we've survived because God has wired us to experience a surge of powerful brain chemicals when we feel threatened, and these chemicals enable us to react more quickly. At this point, very few of us are threatened by saber tooth tigers, but our reaction to unsettling news is much the same as our ancestors'. And in the past year or so, the onslaught of negative, confusing, and contradictory messages—combined with sickness and death of people we know and love—has shifted our amygdala into overdrive!

Every change, even one that promises a better future, is unsettling, especially if it occurs rapidly. We function best when we have a relative sense of peace and security, but pandemics, coupled with economic disruption, shatter our equilibrium.

As leaders, we feel frazzled, so our brain chemistry produces neurotransmitters that make us want to fight, flee, or freeze. The people who live under our roofs and the people we lead are experiencing the same perceived threats, and their reactions fall into the same three categories. If we're not careful, we exacerbate each other's threat level, and together we spiral into blame, resentment, and even more isolation. We need to find a better way to cope.

CARE...MORE THAN EVER

We're problem solvers. We're "make it happen" people. We're the rocks that stand strong in the midst of the storm-tossed waves. Yes, that's the way we want to be viewed in normal times, but maybe even more in the middle of a crisis. When people are afraid, they need one thing more than anything else from us: empathy. They want to know that we understand what they're feeling, how they're thinking, and the fears that cloud their minds each day. And one more thing: they want to know that we're human and experience the same fears they do.

Let me offer a few suggestions:

BE REAL

You don't have to tell your people about every fear and heartache, but it's wise to open the window on your soul to a significant degree. When they realize you're "one of them," defenses will come down, expectations will be more realistic, and understanding will smooth the way in conversations about planning and implementation.

JUDGE NOT

The often-quoted verse from Jesus's Sermon on the Mount (see Matthew 7:1) doesn't mean we're not allowed to analyze people and situations; it means we don't harshly condemn them—especially when their emotional margins have been eroded by fears and doubts during the pandemic. Instead of jumping in to correct a person's thinking and reactions, take time to listen, really listen, and affirm the fact that everyone is under a lot of pressure.

FLEX...BUT JUST A LITTLE

We need to show flexibility without losing all semblance of order. During and after the pandemic, people face demands that are out of the realm of normal. Many have been working remotely from home at the same time their children are in school virtually...and the little kids need continual supervision. In addition, sick family members require time and attention, and if your employees can't go to the hospital to be with them, they feel the added burden of grief on top of their worries.

Empathy is a soft skill—an essential soft skill. It matters to the people we lead. In a *Forbes* article, "Why Empathy Is Vital for Effective Leadership, Especially in Times of Crisis," Kim Pope says, "Organizations with leadership teams that lack empathy have high staff turnover rates. After all, who wants to work for a company that doesn't understand how they feel and is unable to support their needs?" She reports that 82 percent of employees "would consider leaving their job for a more empathetic organization" and 78 percent "would work longer hours for a more empathetic employer."[8]

EMPATHY IS A SOFT SKILL—AN ESSENTIAL SOFT SKILL. IT MATTERS TO THE PEOPLE WE LEAD.

Employees value leaders who care about them.

David Schwimmer, CEO of London Stock Exchange Group, says, "People are looking to me for a different kind of leadership. In a normal environment, it's about business leadership and setting up strategy, as well as culture and people decisions. In this environment, it's about helping people maintain morale. It's about people being prepared for whatever may come in the face of uncertainty." And Steve Collis, CEO of AmerisourceBergen, remarks, "One of the smartest things that we did the very first week was to set up a daily executive-management meeting at 5:00 p.m. That's important from a decision-making point of view, but it's even more important for touching base and showing empathy. We're now in each other's homes—you're seeing my study, and we've met each other's families.…I asked all my direct reports, 'Is there someone who wants me to reach out to someone who's doing a great job or someone who's struggling? Maybe someone who has a relative with COVID-19?' Sometimes all that's needed is a word of encouragement to show you care. It's been a great gift to be able to do that for the people in AmerisourceBergen."[9]

My advice for all of us is clear: go and do likewise.

AMID THE DISTRACTIONS

Like the cleanup efforts after a hurricane, the months and years after the pandemic require us to incorporate new insights about leadership, but at the same time, we need to retain what's most important. We'll often wonder, *Where do I begin? What's most important? What's wasting my time? What do people need from me now—right now?* In the reorientation of life and work, keep these things in mind:

STRENGTHEN YOUR CORE

Your leadership team needs you more than ever. Make fewer assumptions about their mental and emotional health, and care for them in powerful ways. Make empathy a "must do" on your priority list.

STAY FOCUSED ON YOUR CALLING

In every kind of organization, a lot has changed, but not the primary calling. In business, it's to serve customers with integrity and quality. In churches, it's still to lead people to a saving knowledge of Christ and help them grow in their faith. In nonprofits, it's to marshal community resources to care for the disadvantaged and serve them in ways that connect with their hearts as you provide tangible services.

STAY CALM

I'm afraid that sheer self-effort to keep everything under control doesn't work very well for the vast majority of us (or any of us). To experience peace in the midst of crashing waves, we need to find a source of unshakable strength, joy, and love.

PROVIDE CLEAR DIRECTION

In the chaos of the storm and in the long, laborious cleanup, our role as leaders is to be the voice that says, "I'm here. I'm for you. Come with me." We may not have everything figured out, but we can give people a lot of assurance when we let them know we're doing our best to find the right way forward.

Yes, we're stretched thin. Yes, we have our own worries and fears. And yes, we're not sure about what's coming next. But we're leaders, and leaders lead. We may have to dig deeper than ever before, trust God for more wisdom than we've ever had, and care more obviously than we ever thought necessary. And if we do, the people we lead will not only weather the storm, they'll absorb values and lessons they can use the rest of their lives.

TAKEAWAYS

+ In a crisis, the organizational chart may be turned upside down.

+ There is a pandemic within the pandemic.

+ More than ever, leaders need to find the inner strength to demonstrate empathy.

THINK ABOUT IT

1. During the pandemic, who did you rely on who may have been on the periphery of your organization before? What have you appreciated about the contribution of these people? Where would your business, church, or nonprofit be without them?

2. How have you seen evidence of "the pandemic within the pandemic"? Which of the statistics in that part of the chapter (if any) surprised you? What will you do to address these wounds?

3. Who in your organization has shown remarkable empathy during the struggle and exiting the pandemic? What have you learned from that person or those people?

4. What steps can you take right away to strengthen your core (your team), reinforce your sense of calling, find a source of peace so you can stay calm in the middle of the distractions and pressures, and provide clear direction for your people?

5

THE PROCESS OF CHANGE

Losing your head in a crisis is a good way
to become a crisis.
—C. J. Redwine, bestselling author

The CEO of a major organization laughed when he told me, "Sam, right now I'm trying to change the fan belt on my car while I'm driving down the highway at full speed!" He saw me smile, so he tried another one on me: "I'm sewing the parachute after I've jumped out of the burning plane!"

I knew exactly what he was saying. The pace of change has accelerated, people are stressed out in many different ways, and the process of making decisions is driven far more by instinct and educated guesses because confusion and ambiguity have replaced the normal patterns of analysis, vetting ideas, limited experiments to test the concept, and an orchestrated rollout.

During the pandemic, the questions have come fast and furiously, and often with conflicting guidance...or unforeseen delays. For instance, if a CEO or a pastor has fifty employees, a common set of questions that had to be answered in a heartbeat might include:

+ How many of our people can work from home, and how many need to be on-site?

+ How can we reach our customers and those who attend our services so they stay involved and we stay relevant?

+ How do we help parents whose children are out of school?

+ What about those who refuse to send their children back to school when it opens?

+ How can we get our people vaccinated as quickly as possible?

+ What about those who refuse to be vaccinated? Will we allow them to remain employed or attend worship?

+ Should we take a stand on masks, social distancing, and vaccinations? What if we don't?

+ How will we relate to people who value personal freedom over public safety?

+ What should I put on social media? Who should monitor our social media?

+ How should we respond to posts that criticize me and our corporate decisions?

+ How can I appear to be credible and in control when I feel so out of control?

+ As the process of reopening progresses and people demand a faster return to normal, how will we address their impatience?

The questions can be endless.

REEVALUATING

As change agents, leaders have a carefully constructed and frequently rehearsed process of decision-making. Over years if not decades, we've practiced this process and seen the benefits in those we trust for input and feedback, the timing, and the benefits and repercussions of particular decisions. Countless experiences have ingrained these processes in our minds so that we don't even need to think about them—they've become second nature. Dr. Tim Elmore, the founder and CEO of Growing Leaders, calls this "unconscious competence." He identifies four distinct stages of competence: unconscious incompetence (we don't know what we don't know); conscious incompetence (we know what we don't know); conscious competence (we're aware of what we know); and unconscious competence (we aren't even aware of all we know).[1] When we get to this final stage, we have a sixth sense about the way particular people will respond, how long it will take for people to get on board, the timing of implementation, and so on. We're thinking, but at a subconscious level.

We might use two very different metaphors to illustrate the built-in, established decision-making processes. When a rancher releases a herd of cattle into a new pasture, the cows, bulls, and calves immediately realize the location of the water source and the bales of hay. They may graze over the entire pasture, but in only a few days, the cattle have trampled clear paths to these two places, and over time, the paths get more clearly defined.

Another metaphor is at the other end of the spectrum: when you and I go online, we see ads that correspond with what we've purchased before or at least looked at. Everything we've clicked on becomes part of our digital fingerprint, and as we look at the new ads, our profile is self-reinforcing.

That's what happens in our planning process. We use a method, it works, it's affirmed by others, and the feedback of people and the success of events reinforces our framework. Soon, we're not even aware that we were intentional at the beginning. Our process is then based on internal, established assumptions.

WE HAVE TO LEARN TO NAVIGATE IN THE TURBULENT SEAS OF AMBIGUITY.

In a crisis, all (or at least many) of these assumptions are blown away like dry autumn leaves caught up in a driving wind. We have to learn to navigate in the turbulent seas of ambiguity. Or to use yet another metaphor, suddenly, the earth has shifted on its axis. People have moved a notch or two down the acquiescence spectrum because change makes them feel more uncomfortable. So, those who were eager to get on board are now hesitant, those who had normally been hesitant are defiant, and those who had been defiant...well, it's best to stay clear from them!

The pace of change and the process of change are inextricably related. The compressed timeframe for decisions forces leaders to use a more streamlined process. Time consuming analysis and studies take far too much time, so leaders have to prioritize their sources of input and make the best decision in the time allotted. If they wait too long, their people will wonder if their leader is on top of things, and he loses credibility. (He's also likely to receive ornery emails and texts.)

During and after a crisis, leaders have to rethink the fundamental elements of their organizations, such as:

+ How you organize

+ How you connect with your team

+ How you relate to people outside the organization

+ How you measure success

+ How you use your facilities

+ How you handle finances

In pressurized times, we sense intuitively who we can count on for quick and insightful feedback, which is preferable, or we determine by trial and error, which is effective but takes longer and is messy. Those who were adept at prolonged, careful, detailed analysis sometimes feel confused and annoyed by the leader's new process. They soon eliminate themselves from the essential core of the leader's most trusted lieutenants. As I mentioned earlier, the swift changes in strategy flip the organizational chart upside down, so people who had previously served on the margins become central to the leader's plans. Will the organizational chart right itself and return to normal after the pandemic? Maybe, at least to some degree, but probably not entirely. During the crisis, leaders have learned how to reach their audience and customers in new, effective ways, and those ways will still be effective when the crush of rapid change subsides.

IN TIMES OF CRISIS, THE EFFECTS OF CHANGE ARE MULTIPLIED BECAUSE RAPID SHIFTS ARE HAPPENING BOTH OUTSIDE AND INSIDE THE ORGANIZATION.

BACK TO BASICS

In the best of times, change is disruptive. In times of crisis, the effects of change are multiplied because rapid shifts are happening both outside and inside the organization. In these times, we need to remember the fundamental truths about change:

1. *All change is a critique of the past.*

It at least implies that the way things used to be needs to be updated, but often, it means the old ways need to be overhauled or replaced.

2. *All change affects people personally, so it's always taken personally.*

Change is never merely academic or purely objective. It's always subjective, so people feel the change as much as (or more than) they conceptualize it.

3. *All change is perceived as loss.*

Leaders instigate change so the organization can grow, but people are emotionally connected to the status quo. Some measure of grief is an inevitable part of change.

4. All change needs a "champion."

This is usually the primary leader who is willing to expend personal equity for the good of the organization. Without this person, plans quickly become diluted and momentum is lost.

5. All change has casualties.

"Blood on the floor" is unavoidable. Some losses are very painful for at least some of the people. Leaders who aren't willing to push forward abdicate their roles.

6. All change will be misunderstood.

You can control your decision but not how people respond to it. Count on it: a few people will make wrong—and sometimes absurd—assumptions about your ideas, your motives, and your sanity.

7. Not everyone will be happy.

Most change agents feel the pressing need for everyone to understand, agree, and affirm. However, that's a completely unrealistic expectation that will consume the leader's time and attention as he tries to make everyone happy, which delays progress.

8. All change is about getting worse before getting better.

Exercise makes your muscles feel weaker, but it's actually making them stronger. If we have little endurance, we'll remain weak.

9. All change needs a "transition plan."

It is transitional issues, not the change, that come back and bite if they're not handled well. There's a significant difference. Change is external; it happens whether people agree or coordinate with it. Transition is internal; it's the new thinking, deeper motivations, and greater buy-in to the plans.

10. Change imposed is change opposed.

Some leaders are bold and decisive, but they may not be sensitive to the way new plans affect people. Others are compassionate, but they may not be willing to launch initiatives that upset others. The very best leaders are both bold and compassionate, pressing ahead while patiently bringing people along with them.

Perception is reality. In other words, if we have unrealistic expectations of how people will respond, our wrong perceptions will cause us to be reactive. But if we anticipate the complexities of making changes in our organizations, we won't be thrown for a loop when they happen. Again, let's be ruthlessly honest about the reality of leading in a crisis: we feel more pressured, and our people feel more anxious. More than ever, we need to be realistic.

LET'S BE RUTHLESSLY HONEST ABOUT THE REALITY OF LEADING IN A CRISIS: WE FEEL MORE PRESSURED, AND OUR PEOPLE FEEL MORE ANXIOUS. MORE THAN EVER, WE NEED TO BE REALISTIC.

A REVISED PROCESS

To carve a new decision-making process in times of crisis, most of us need to make at least some minor adjustments to the way we've done things in the past—and some of us need to make some major revisions. Let me offer four suggestions that will be instrumental in navigating the post-pandemic world.

TOLERATE AMBIGUITY

Life has always had a degree of uncertainty, but the pandemic shook many of our preconceptions about the structured and predictable way organizations normally operate. Leaders who demand to have all the answers before taking steps have been—and will continue to be—at a distinct disadvantage.

In an article entitled "Six problem-solving mindsets for very uncertain times," Charles Conn and Robert McLean recommend new strategies during and after a crisis, and they encourage leaders to embrace the unknowns:

> When we think of problem solvers, many of us tend to picture a poised and brilliant engineer. We may imagine a mastermind who knows what she's doing and approaches a problem with purpose. The reality, though, is that most good problem solving has a lot of trial and error; it's more like the apparent randomness of rugby than the precision of linear programming. We form hypotheses, porpoise into the data, and then surface and refine (or throw out) our initial guess at the answer. This above all requires an embrace of imperfection and a tolerance for ambiguity—and a gambler's sense of probabilities.[2]

You may not think of yourself as a gambler, but when we have to pivot quickly to make decisions, each one carries a higher degree of risk than the ones that are the product of our usual, more carefully considered processes.

ASK MORE QUESTIONS...AND LISTEN

The rush to adjust during the pandemic shifted our perception of the go-to people who could quickly make necessary changes, and it forced many employees to find creative ways to accomplish their roles. As the pandemic subsides, wise leaders will ask questions about each person's role, what they've learned from the changes during the pandemic, and how they can collaborate more effectively. This global corporate reassessment may well result in a very different organizational chart, greater collaboration, and structural changes in roles, reporting, and goals.

VALUE THOSE WHO HAVE PROVEN TO BE REMARKABLY PERCEPTIVE

You already know who they are, don't you? In the past couple of years, they had insights no one else conceived, they saw opportunity where others saw disaster, and they had a vision of the changes that should be implemented while others remained confused and passive. We need to surround ourselves with people like this, or find at least one person who has this level of insight. We probably became leaders because we proved we're skilled at particular aspects of our roles, and there's nothing wrong with that! But as we lead our organizations into the future, we need people who have an uncanny ability to see what others don't.

PAY ATTENTION TO THE CROWD

Chris Bradley, coauthor of *Strategy Beyond the Hockey Stick*, observes, "It's a mistake to think that on your team you have the smartest people in the room. They aren't there. They're invariably somewhere else."[3] If we've learned anything from the digital revolution, it's that people are more than willing to give us feedback, if we'll only ask. Crowdsourcing isn't just for Internet companies; it can be an effective tool for all leaders. Of course, not all input is equally valuable, but the fact that someone took time to communicate with us tells us they're interested in our organizations. People on the outside aren't hindered by "the way things work around here," so they're free to let their creativity fly.

Some of us aren't comfortable being challenged by people we don't know (and therefore don't respect). Get over it! Talk to your young IT people, and ask them to formulate a strategy to reach out to people beyond your walls. If you do, you'll accomplish at least two things: your IT staff will feel deeply valued; and you'll gather a wealth of input from people who can become your audience or customer base. Not bad...not bad at all.

Aaron Dignan, founder of The Ready, coaches executives in organizational transformation. He summarizes the way leaders need to respond to the changes we now face:

> We need to go faster. Be more innovative. Make better decisions—waste less time. Break down silos. Work horizontally. Simplify our structure. Focus on the customer. Increase information flow. Scale without losing what makes us great. Change our business model. Attract different talent. Retain the great talent we have.[4]

This is a season for the brave and the creative. Be that kind of leader.

TAKEAWAYS

+ We need to reevaluate our second-nature, well-rehearsed decision-making pathways.

+ Responses to change are more extreme during a crisis, so we need to be realistic about our expectations of ourselves and others.

+ The process we revise now will pay dividends long after the pressure subsides.

THINK ABOUT IT

1. How would you describe your decision-making process before the pandemic? How did it change when the crisis began?

2. What do you think it means to "become comfortable with ambiguity"? Who do you know who has that level of comfort with the unknown...and is a very effective leader?

3. What are some reasons it's important to remember the fundamental truths about people's reactions to change as we navigate the crisis and after it's over?

4. Which of the four elements of a revised strategy is the highest priority for you to implement? What difference will it make?

6

PROGRAMS IN CHANGE

The art of progress is to preserve order amid change
and preserve change amid order.
—Alfred North Whitehead,
English mathematician and philosopher

In 2020, I was invited to speak at four conferences in Europe, two in Dubai, four in India, two in New Zealand, two in Australia, and several more in South America. In my career as a consultant, I've responded to these invitations by preparing my messages, booking flights, and traveling to the events where thousands of leaders came to hear me speak. I enjoyed casual interactions with people who coordinated the events and those who attended. I often had the chance to visit amazing sites in those countries with my hosts as my tour guides.

Suddenly, in late February of that year, all of these events were cancelled, postponed, or put on hold indefinitely. Some of the coordinators were optimistic, hoping the pandemic would subside fairly quickly, but of course it didn't. It only got worse. In the end, none of the events happened. We still had some, but we had them online. And instead of thousands sitting in an auditorium rubbing shoulders with other leaders, I looked at a few dozen boxes containing people's images on my computer screen.

Programming is about delivery systems. It puts people together so they can learn, worship, sell, buy, and negotiate. During the pandemic, leaders of every type of organization had to find ways to connect with people. As we've seen, the leaders often received conflicting (or at least confusing) directives from government agencies, so they closed, opened, partially closed, opened a bit more, closed completely, and then gradually reopened again. In each phase, they had to reassess their programs so they could connect effectively with leadership teams, employees, customers, volunteers, and members.

Even before the pandemic, leaders realized they had to capitalize on the online opportunities—or be left behind. Virtually every organization was ramping up online marketing and services, and we're not the only ones who are interested in the data. Alarmingly, biotech companies and those that analyze a person's ancestry by DNA have acquired an enormous amount of information about each person who participates—estimated at 50 million at this point. In an expose by

60 Minutes, reporter Jon Wertheim interviewed FBI Special Agent Edward You. Genealogy companies market their DNA analysis as an interesting consumer product. You explained:

> The return on investment is aggregating the data and what they can do with it once they have enough of it.… The value is in the data. It—it's not just the genealogy companies. Everybody is looking at what kind of data do I have access to, how much do I have, and then how can I turn around and—and monetize it.…Data is the new oil—and it's all types of health data that might come from your smart-watch, your social media, your credit card.[1]

PARADOXICALLY, DATA IS MAKING OUR LIVES FAR MORE CONNECTED TO INFORMATION BUT LESS CONNECTED TO OTHER PEOPLE.

Data is transforming our world just as much as oil transformed mobility, energy for our homes and offices, plastics, and virtually every other aspect of our lives. Oil enabled us to drive to work, go shopping, take our kids to practice and games, go to church, and see parts of the country that only the very wealthy had time and money enough to visit. In other words, the programming of human life was utterly revolutionized by the use of oil—and it's currently being revolutionized by data. Paradoxically, data is making our lives far more connected to information but less connected to other people.

A QUICK PIVOT

Before the pandemic, we were already making the gradual move to data-driven programs, but COVID forced leaders to make a hard, sharp pivot in that direction. Elementary schools are a classic case of the challenges posed by this change. When schools closed, learning became a virtual experience, but teachers had no experience with this kind of communication, and the kids' attention spans proved to be as substantive as a wisp of smoke. It was challenging enough keeping little children engaged with the teachers during in-class learning; it proved to be incredibly difficult online. Parents were often working from home, so their attention was split between their work and keeping their children connected with their teachers. Parents sometimes took on more of the teaching responsibilities to make up for the lack of classroom connections, but few parents were skilled at teaching "new math" to their grade school children. The kids missed their friends, and the parents missed some peace and quiet.

The content of the classroom was the same—reading, writing, arithmetic, history, geography, social sciences, and so on—but the delivery system was radically different. During 2020, there were fiercely conflicting opinions about a lot of things, such as the usefulness of masks and the availability of testing and vaccines, but perhaps nothing was as emotionally polarizing as opening schools for in-classroom teaching. Many parents needed their kids to go back to school so they could return to work—an economic necessity for those who earned a living on-site—but many teachers feared potential exposure to children who might carry the disease from home to the classroom. The delivery system was of paramount importance to everyone, even as they disagreed on the solution to the problem.

CONSOLIDATE, DON'T DISCARD

As I've mentioned in virtually every chapter, leaders have realized that the pandemic didn't merely create short-term chaos and temporary solutions; it has had a lasting impact on how organizations deliver goods and services. It is certainly our tendency to long to *go back to the way things used to be*, but instead, we need to consolidate the positive, effective programming we implemented during the pandemic. Let me offer some ideas and suggestions:

1. Affirm Your Innovators

Yes, we're tired of the prolonged adrenaline rush that endured during the pandemic. It seemed that something changed every day, but the exact nature of the changes remained frustratingly uncertain. Urgency prompted us to be creative to look for solutions to problems we didn't even know existed—and we learned to value people who brought us innovative answers. Now, on the backside of the pandemic, it's not time to dust off the old programs and implement them again. The world has shifted, and wise leaders shift with it. "Elevate the innovators" is a good leadership slogan for the next phase of our organizations.

"ELEVATE THE INNOVATORS" IS A GOOD LEADERSHIP SLOGAN FOR THE NEXT PHASE OF OUR ORGANIZATIONS.

In an article entitled "Forcing Change: Driving Innovation and Delivering Results," Brett Ridge and Brian Reich specifically address leaders of nonprofit organizations, but their principles apply to leaders of all organizations: "So often, nonprofits have a strong base of committed volunteers, but fail to use them in the area of innovation. By learning how to best leverage volunteers, organizations can build their credibility and reach while gaining new ideas, solutions, and energy that are so critical to success. In many cases, this means having the right person in the right job at the right place and time. The key is to find smart people with passion. Have faith that their excellence, when applied properly, not only helps the organization's efforts, but also creates an opportunity for others to distinguish themselves and find solutions."[2] Why? Because innovation is contagious!

2. Make the Vision Bite-Sized

We've learned many things in the months when we had to find instant solutions to new problems, and one of the most important was that it was easy for us to be distracted and our vision to be diluted by all the new challenges. Now, as we come out of the pressure cooker, it's smart to reaffirm the *why* of our organizations as we restructure the *who, what, when,* and *how.* Each person on the team needs a bite of the vision apple, something each one can achieve that will reinforce individual responsibilities and celebrate contributions as the organization aims high again. The organizational chart may look very different now, but vision, delegation, and follow-up are still essential, and perhaps even more important as we change our delivery systems.

3. Get the Very Best From Each Person

Leadership is about bringing people with us to reach a goal that's far bigger than we could achieve on our own. Programs were revised during the pandemic and are being analyzed after it, and each person on the team can play a major role in the new look of the organization. Redouble your efforts to invite collaboration, to value input that's outside the box, affirm contributions, and point people to the larger vision—and don't hesitate to ask for their best efforts. The changes your organization experienced shouldn't be wasted. Learn from them, think bigger, and value people who invest themselves in doing the seemingly impossible. Empower those who have shown promise, even if they haven't had a primary slot on the organizational chart. This probably requires a change in their job descriptions so they can devote their newly appreciated talents to the role you envision for them.

4. Use Multiple Touch Points

During the pandemic, we had to find new delivery systems—or at least switch our priorities from one to another. As the culture becomes more data-driven, we need to utilize every possible touch point, not just in-person connections, but also podcasts, videos, and the full range of virtual platforms.

5. Stay Optimistic

The first months of the pandemic created a sense of urgency, which caused some people to panic but energized others to be incredibly creative. As the months wore on, however, even many of the most hopeful suffered under the daily grind of trying to inject hope into people who felt confused, sad, and resentful that life wasn't returning to normal as fast as they expected. To be sure, there were plenty of headaches and heartaches, but some people in our organizations rose to the challenge and served with confidence and excellence. It's important for us to leverage all the gains we made in our creative programming and manage the very real losses we suffered. People looked to us for comfort and hope during COVID, and they look to us now to make sense of what happened and for direction into the future.

Business management expert John Kotter recognizes that it's very easy for organizations to take two steps forward and then two steps back to the status quo. He offers this advice for leaders who implement new systems: "At first, changes are fragile. They need nourishment and protection in order to take root in the organization. Be vigilant of hard-fought changes, and recognize that many of them will take years to be fully ingrained in the organization. The best leaders know change is not a once-in-a-while proposition. The process of change is ongoing. When leaders manage change effectively, they gain respect and earn the right to craft a culture where change is a regular, even welcome, aspect of the organization."[3]

If you implement these ideas, I believe you'll create new delivery systems and fine-tune some that have worked well.

USE A PENCIL

As we figure out how to apply the lessons we learned from the pandemic, we need a shot of humility in our planning. Use a pencil with a good eraser because the one thing we can be certain of is uncertainty. We're in a time of change, and many of the parameters we used before in our planning process will need to be updated.

Use a pencil with a good eraser because the one thing we can be certain of is uncertainty.

I've read that it's wise for leaders to create contingency plans, but in my experience as a consultant, I've noticed that when leaders create contingency plans, they quickly become wedded to them. The word *contingent* is meant to imply flexibility, but the written plans are interpreted as permanent. Heavyweight boxer Mike Tyson famously said, "Everybody has a plan until they get punched in the face." In the pandemic, we've all been punched in the face many times!

I'm not advocating that we shouldn't plan. We should, but we need to realize that contingency plans must remain *contingent*. If we have a Plan B, we need to be open to Plans C through at least G. Some critical factors in these plans include:

+ *What we know is true.*

Including those we can count on, the systems that are currently working, the rock-solid vision for the future, and the values that guide our operations.

+ *What don't we know and how long won't we know?*

Such as who will come back to the office when the pandemic is over, who won't, how we can reach them most effectively, the financial implications of any change in plans, the programs that can be reinstituted, those that need to be changed, and those to be abandoned.

+ *Who should be involved in this flexible planning strategy?*

Including those who have shown remarkable creativity with new ideas to solve problems, gatekeepers who affect many others in the organization, and/or a restructured leadership team.

+ *Who should be involved in quick decisions and implementation?*

Consider changes to the system so fewer people are included in the process, but communicate clearly so that everyone will be involved in implementation.

+ *How to communicate a change of plans, showing confidence in the direction but with appropriate humility and flexibility.*

Think about the ways people get information and use digital platforms to communicate, but keep in mind there will also be those who don't have access to these platforms, so devise a strategy to connect with them.

+ *How to construct a feedback loop that works as plans are in flux.*

Consider that even though the decision-making process is faster and fewer people are involved in that process, it's perhaps even more important to get accurate feedback from customers and constituents. Craft a way for people to respond so you know what's working and what's not.

+ *How to define success.*

In times of significant change, success may be defined by the number of people you retain as loyal customers, clients, members, and attendees, or perhaps revenue and market share, as well as the morale of your team. However, for many organizations, simply making it to the other side is a major accomplishment!

GRACE UNDER PRESSURE

When we're stressed, we have an urge to react instead of respond, to be emotional instead of rational. For years, we counted on our programs to carry our message and create environments where people would want what we offer, but in a crisis, these programs become threatened...and maybe irrelevant. It's easy to let the moment get the best of us, and even the most gifted of us have moments of weakness. In an article for Korn Ferry, Gary Burnison shares his response to pressure and the lesson he's learning. First, one of the most important leadership virtues is radical honesty:

> Despite my best intentions, a couple of weeks ago during a conversation with a colleague I just lost it. I had asked this person to do something and, when it wasn't done, I immediately jumped to conclusions. I slipped into command-and-control mode and let my anger get the best of me. After reflecting on how poorly that conversation had gone, I called the person first thing the next morning to apologize: "I'm sorry. I didn't listen to what you were saying." In that moment, I could just sense the person's body language shifting—like letting out a breath. No matter how much we try to get things right, we'll usually get things wrong. It takes humility and vulnerability to admit those failings, first to ourselves and then to others.[4]

Burnison learned to practice "urgent patience":

> **Urgent patience is a virtue:** Impatience doesn't get the job done. It inspires more fear than high performance, which can override critical thinking. Anybody who has gone into a skid on black ice can relate: your instinct is to slam on the brakes and jerk the wheel in the opposite direction. It takes a clear head to do the opposite—the counterintuitive—of steering into the

skid to regain control. It's time for leaders to "ease up on the stick," too. Urgent patience is the real virtue here. Or, in the words of Emperor Augustus, *"Festina lente"*—make haste slowly. It's the grace under pressure that turns crisis into opportunity.[5]

A crisis shakes our sense of equilibrium, causes us to question our hold on things, and forces us to face questions we'd never asked before. Before the crisis, we fussed over our delivery systems to fine-tune them, but during the shake up, we had to make decisions on the fly to figure out how to keep the ship afloat. More than a year's worth of change has affected us as leaders, our teams, and the people we serve—and the change will last. Our task is to change with it and recreate our programs for the future.

TAKEAWAYS

+ Programs are simply delivery systems for our message and the environments we want to create.

+ The systems we created during the pandemic will certainly affect the way we do business and the church in the future.

+ Contingency plans are...well, contingent.

THINK ABOUT IT

1. When the pandemic began to affect your organization, what were the first changes to your delivery systems? How did these continue to morph during the months of shutdowns and openings?

2. In what way is data "the new oil" for your organization? Or is it?

3. Who are the people in your organization who have had innovative ideas about reframing your delivery systems? Which of these changes will become permanent?

4. Do you feel comfortable being flexible with your planning? Explain your answer.

5. What does (or would) "urgent patience" look like in your leadership?

7

PROCLAMATION IN CHANGE

The challenge of leadership is to be strong, but not
rude; be kind, but not weak; be bold, but not bully;
be thoughtful, but not lazy; be humble, but not
timid; be proud, but not arrogant.
—Jim Rohn,
author, entrepreneur, and motivational speaker

Every leader at *every* level in *every* organization is effective
only to the extent that their communication is clear and com-
pelling. These leaders make their mark by proclaiming blends
of vision and compassion, direction and hope, challenge and
patience. When the pandemic hit and many people began
working from home, leaders had to use a different medium

to communicate. In-person, face-to-face connections were instantly replaced with Zoom and other video conferencing tools. At first, this novel approach was kind of exciting, but after a while, leaders realized their people had difficulty concentrating, the message wasn't as clear as they thought, and they missed the opportunities to talk before and after meetings—encounters that proved to be very important but had been taken for granted before COVID.

Leaders realized their primary proclamation task was no longer the dissemination of concepts; it was finding ways to connect with their people so they still felt they were valued members of the team. Communication focuses on content; connecting is about empathy. Communication describes the organization's direction; connecting values each person. The shift was from projects to people. You might say, "But Sam, we always communicated that our people are important." I'd answer, "Yes, I'm sure you did, but it's a matter of focus, emphasis, and impact. When you were together before, during, and after a meeting, you could make assumptions about the depth and quality of the relationships. During the pandemic when your team met only for short periods on screens, those assumptions went out the window."

ADDRESSING THE ELEPHANT

The leader of a large organization told me, "It didn't take long. In the first couple of weeks when our team was at home and our meetings were online, everyone looked like they did when they came to the office. They wore the nice clothes they always wore at work, the women had obviously fixed their hair and put on makeup, and the guys had brushed their hair. Their facial hair was carefully cut to look relaxed and manly—you know what I mean, don't you?"

I assured him I did. I wanted to say, "Are you looking at me right now? That's the look I'm trying to achieve, even if I'm a few decades older than the sharp young men in your organization." But I didn't mention that.

He continued, "But before long, I noticed some changes: They began to wear workout clothes, the women hadn't made any attempts to freshen up, and the beards...let's just say the guys must not have looked in the mirror before we met. Some came prepared with research and data I'd assigned them to get for us, but others had excuses for being unprepared. Then, a week or two later, some of them looked like they had just finished their exercise regimen—sweat rolled down their faces. A few of them were late to get on the calls, and it appeared that many of them were distracted during the meetings. I hoped it was emails related to our topic of conversation, but since they didn't add any new ideas they had gotten from their distractions, I'm pretty sure they were on Facebook, Instagram, Twitter, and other social media...or maybe they were shopping for new gym clothes or ordering takeout. I don't know what they were doing, but...Sam, have you heard the term 'herding cats'? That became my management style during these meetings. It was all I could do to keep them engaged in our conversation."

I asked, "So, did you find a way to make this method work?"

He smiled, "Yes, I stopped in the middle of one of our meetings and asked them, 'Do you see any difference in how we related in these online calls when we started and now?' After some painful silence, several of them admitted they hadn't been 'all there' after the first week or two. It was a necessary wakeup conversation for our team, and we did better after that. Don't get me wrong: it was still difficult to keep everyone engaged, but we had at least addressed the elephant in the room."

ONE LEADER TOLD ME, "I JUST LISTENED. I DIDN'T TRY TO BE THE FIXER-IN-CHIEF. I WANTED TO BE MORE OF A FRIEND AND ENCOURAGER."

After this leader shared his story with me, I asked other CEOs and pastors to tell me how they were coping with their staff working from home. One of them told me, "When we went over our normal agenda items, our calls had become as dry as toast, so I decided to do something about it. I set up weekly video chats with two or three of them at a time—just to connect with them person to person...no tasks, no projects, no reports, no pressure. Each time, I simply asked, 'How are you doing? How's your family? What are the struggles you're experiencing during this crazy time?' And I just listened. I didn't try to be the fixer-in-chief. I wanted to be more of a friend and encourager. They needed my support more than I had imagined... but you know, that's on me. I should have put myself in their shoes long before I did."

Instantly, I realized this was a brilliant leadership move. A week later, I was on a call with the pastor of a South African church with about 20,000 people on the rolls. I told him about the insight I'd learned from the leader who carved out time to connect with his people on a personal level, and we discussed the massive undertaking it would mean for his church to do something similar. He landed on a strategy to recruit and train kind, compassionate leaders and give them fifty people to care for during the rest of the pandemic. They called two people each day so everyone received a touch point at least once a month. Later, he told me, "Sam, it was amazing! I'm sure a few people fell through the cracks and didn't feel cared for, but the vast majority of people have reported that these heartfelt connections have meant the world to them during this difficult time. Somebody cared for them personally. They were no longer a statistic—they felt loved. It changed the people in our church from borderline resentment and self-pity to partners in the adventure of weathering the COVID storm!"

THE SECOND MILE

When the pandemic began and pastors had only days to switch from in-person worship to online, most of them live-streamed their services at the regular service times. It made perfect sense—people were used to going to church at those hours on Sunday mornings. Soon, however, pastors posted their services on YouTube and other media platforms, and people began worshipping on demand when it was convenient for them.

Again, this made sense, but I believe it's a sign that people are less emotionally connected with the pastor, the worship team, and the broader church. They click on the church service in the same way they'd watch a movie on Netflix or a comedian on YouTube. Please don't misunderstand: I'm thrilled that they take the initiative to worship online, but the on-demand style tells me the church is becoming more of a commodity for them than a vital source of faith, hope, and love. Hopefully, their joy will rekindle when they worship together in church again.

We shouldn't underestimate the importance of casual conversations people have before and after in-person services. They see their friends, they check on someone they've prayed for, and they make eye contact with people who have similar beliefs and values. In other words, they feel they're part of a wider community. When they download a worship service at home, it's much more difficult to impart that sense of community, but it's essential for pastors and worship teams to try.

Leaders need to enter the world of their people, to share their own heartaches and struggles of isolation, and share those stories as part of the on-demand worship services. For instance, a pastor might say, "As many of you know, John Doe died last week. I've known and loved John for many years, and I'll miss him a lot. We held his funeral on Wednesday. There were only ten of us in the room, but a number of you joined us on live stream. It's hard to say goodbye to someone we love, and for many of you, it was painful to say goodbye on a computer screen. Someday, we'll be together again, but for now, I want you to know that our love for each other hasn't diminished at all—our ability to be in the same room has changed, but our love hasn't."

Another pastor shared with his people, "As many of you know, social distancing and quarantining has made life very difficult for my family. My mother has been in the hospital for a week. She has COVID, and a few days ago, the doctors put her on a ventilator. I can't be with her, and that hurts a lot. I go to the hospital and sit in the parking lot and pray for her. It's as close as I can get, and for now, it's all I can do. Thank you for joining me in prayer for her. It means so much that you care for her, too."

Sometimes, members of the wider community step up in remarkable ways. A CBS report described the story of John and Jennifer Schoffstall from a small town in rural Indiana where John was a fireman. When he got sick with COVID, Jennifer couldn't visit him in the hospital. To be near John,

Jennifer and others in her family sat in their car in the hospital parking lot all day and all night for several days. One day, she sent a text to one of the firefighters that she would be at the hospital praying for John that night, and if anyone wanted to join her, they could come at 8 p.m. That night, every fire apparatus engine and every fireman in the town rolled up. The men got out of their vehicles and joined Jennifer in a prayer vigil that lasted for more than a week. On Easter Sunday morning just as the sun was rising, Jennifer was with John on FaceTime when he died. She'll never forget the kindness and dedication of those firemen.[1]

This is the kind of story that connects with people. It's the kind of story all of us need to hear because it taps into our deep need for love and compassion when we're brokenhearted.

OUR PEOPLE NEED US TO GO BEYOND WHAT WE MIGHT THINK IS GOOD AND NECESSARY AND NORMAL. THEY NEED US TO PROCLAIM STORIES THAT CONNECT WITH THEIR HOPES AND FEARS, THEIR VERY REAL PAIN AND WORRIES, AND THEIR NEED FOR SOMEONE TO UNDERSTAND THEM.

Jesus said, *"If anyone forces you to go one mile, go with him two miles"* (Matthew 5:41). That's the spirit of what leaders need to do now in connecting with their people. They need us to go beyond what we might think is good and necessary and normal. They need us to proclaim stories that connect with their hopes and fears, their very real pain and worries, and their need for someone to understand them.

TEFLON NO LONGER

Let me assure you, content is still important, but the ability to connect on an emotional, personal level is more important than ever. In times of crisis, people aren't looking for the brash, bold, go-for-broke kind of leaders who invite people to follow them as they *charge hell with a squirt gun*. Instead, they're looking for leaders who obviously feel what they feel and care for them. Clarity of direction is still important, but people will follow if they know their leaders connect with their deepest emotions.

The writer to the Hebrews assures us, *"For we do not have a high priest who is unable to sympathize with our weaknesses, but one who in every respect has been tempted as we are, yet without sin"* (Hebrews 4:15). And in his letter to the Philippians, Paul explains how Jesus experienced suffering so we can be sure He understands our pain: *"Have this mind among yourselves, which is yours in Christ Jesus, who, though he was in the form of God, did not count equality with God a thing to be grasped, but emptied himself, by taking the form of a servant, being born in the likeness of men. And being found in human form, he humbled himself by becoming obedient to the point of death, even death on a cross"* (Philippians 2:5–8).

We rightly spend a lot of time focusing on Jesus's divinity, but we shouldn't forget His humanity. He wasn't aloof. He felt what we feel, and He experienced the full range of emotions: He was thrilled when the disciples returned from their missionary trip with amazing stories, He wept at the tomb of Lazarus, He was indignant when the disciples didn't show compassion for children, and He was infinitely kind to people who were considered cultural outcasts.

Some of us have tried very hard to be perceived as "above it all," never thrown off balance, and never letting anyone see us sweat. That's not the model of Jesus at all. He wasn't a Teflon leader. He was thoroughly approachable because people knew He genuinely cared for them. He entered their world (our world!) with strength and humility, truth and grace. That's our task as leaders, too.

My wife Brenda has a lot of pots and pans in our kitchen. Some of them are of the non-stick variety, so they're easy to use and clean. But she has an old iron frying pan that has been seasoned with years of oil and care. The very best meals come from that old pan. Sometimes food sticks to the bottom and the sides, but Brenda scrapes the crusty parts to mix with whatever she's cooking. Sometimes, these bits of food seem to be the most flavorful.

What's your flavor and mine? Do we present ourselves as non-stick, or are we a natural substance that provides a richer flavor? I believe it's time for us to be very real with our people, to demonstrate that we're not above them. We hurt like they hurt, we're confused like they're confused, and we grieve the same kinds of losses they grieve. As we reveal our vulnerabilities, we earn the right to speak words of hope into their despair and light into their darkness.

KNOW THIS; DO THIS

In difficult times, people look to leaders for empathy, honesty, clarity, and action. As you consider your proclamation plan, apply these principles:

1. You Can Never Overcommunicate

In a crisis, many of us have a tendency to undercommunicate because we aren't certain what to say, but people need to hear from us, even if our words mirror the uncertainty they're feeling. In addition, when they're under stress, people are distracted, so they don't hear you, and they often hear what they want to hear (or are afraid to hear). Some are in denial about the implications of the problem, but others are in full panic mode! When you think you've said the same thing too many times, it's probably about right.

2. You're Communicating Rationally, But It's Received Emotionally

As a leader, you're trying to impart concepts, principles, and processes, but many of the people on the receiving end are far more in tune with your pathos than your logos. If you connect with them emotionally, they'll be more willing and able to hear your reasoning.

IF YOU CONNECT WITH YOUR PEOPLE EMOTIONALLY, THEY'LL BE MORE WILLING AND ABLE TO HEAR YOUR REASONING.

---

3. You Can't Control Your People's Responses

You control your decisions and your proclamation of those decisions, but you can't control your people's responses. In a crisis, leaders have to realize that people seem to have cotton stuffed in their ears—and they're pretty sure the cotton is on fire!

4. Develop a Cascading Communication Plan

This practice is simple and effective for major decisions. Communicate with your leadership team and board, and come to a decision. Then, take one or more of them with you (in person or online) to share the decision with the next layer of leaders. After that, take one of the top leaders and one or more of the second layer of leaders to share the decision with the next layer. Keep doing that until it's time to share the decision with the whole organization, and perhaps the public. In each stage, give the leaders who are already on board time to share their enthusiasm for the idea. In this way, both the concept and the buy-in of leaders cascades from one level to the next. And of course, we've learned that we can make this cascade happen more quickly on Zoom or other platforms.

5. Even in a Hurry, Always Strive to Be Clear and Precise

In a crisis, there's always a risk that a decision won't turn out the way we planned, but the bigger risk is being paralyzed and making no decision at all. This balance requires leaders to be both humble and decisive. We might say, "We had two days to analyze the situation and make a decision, and this is what we're doing. Let's go in this direction together. I'm sure we'll make course corrections along the way, but I feel good that we're making the best choice right now." When we play it safe by taking a long time to make a decision, our intention is to make a better one than if we rushed it, but inaction during a crisis creates more uncertainty and distrust among those we lead.

6. Keep Closing the Feedback Loop

More than ever, take nothing for granted. Check in with your leadership team to be sure they know your heart and understand their part in the decisions that have been made. They often have questions they didn't feel free to ask when the pressure was on to make the decision, and it's important for them to voice their concerns. And don't equate their questions with disloyalty. Everyone is on edge, and they may say things that seem a bit threatening. Give them a little room to be human, and they'll probably give you the same grace.

Our proclamation has changed. We make fewer assumptions about people really hearing what we're saying, so we spend more time communicating our hearts as we continue to give direction to the people we lead.

TAKEAWAYS

+ Communication is about content; connection is about people.
+ Go the second mile to show empathy and genuine concern.
+ Assume less; connect more.

THINK ABOUT IT

1. What course corrections did you make in your proclamation to your team and the rest of your people during the pandemic? What did you learn from these experiences?

2. Why is it important to implement a strategy to have personal interactions with each person on your team…and through them to your whole organization? What are some painful things that could happen when we don't do this?

3. What stories of compassion have gripped you during the pandemic? How have you used those to share your heart with your people?

4. Do you feel comfortable being at least a bit vulnerable with your people? What are the risks and rewards?

5. Which of the principles in the last section (Know This; Do This) do you need to implement? What difference will it make?

8

PREPARATION FOR CHANGE

Everyone here has the sense that right now is one of
those moments when we are influencing the future.
—Steve Jobs, co-founder of Apple

Planning and preparation are related, but they're not the same
thing. Let me illustrate: you and I unexpectedly see each other
at the airport. I notice that you're looking into your oversized
carry-on, and I see your thermal underwear, heavy socks, a
wool hat, and a down jacket. My conclusion is that you've prepared to go to somewhere that's really cold, but I don't know
your specific plans—the city you're flying to, the resort where
you're staying, how you'll get there, and how long you'll stay.
You may be meeting friends, you may want to ski or sightsee,

and you may plan to stick to a vegan diet the whole time you're away, but I don't know those things simply by looking at how you've prepared for your trip. If I ask you about the purpose of your trip, you might explain that you just need some time to get away and relax, you visit a group of close friends every year, or you love to cross-country ski. The contents of your suitcase tell me the *kind* of place you're going to visit, but almost nothing of your *particular* plans.

While we're waiting for our flights, I open my carry-on, and you see a bottle of sunscreen, a big floppy hat, T-shirts, shorts, and flip-flops. The way I've prepared tells you that I'm not going to the same destination as you are. Quite the opposite. I have no use for thermal underwear and all the other gear I'd need on a polar expedition like yours.

PREPARATIONS ARE BROAD AND STRATEGIC, FOCUSING ON WHAT AND WHY. PLANNING IS NARROW AND TACTICAL, FOCUSING ON THE SPECIFICS OF WHERE, WHEN, WHO, HOW, AND HOW MUCH.

If you opened your organizational suitcase and invited me to take a look inside, what would it tell me about how you're preparing for the future? Your preparation answers the questions *what* and *why*. Planning focuses on the specifics of *where, when, who, how,* and *how much*. Preparations are broad and strategic; planning is narrow and tactical. These are truths we need to remember:

+ *We never pack for where we've been.*

+ *We never pack for where we are.*

+ *We always pack for where we're going.*

You might ask me, "How long did it take you to *plan* the outline for this chapter?"

I'd respond, "About three hours."

And you'd ask, "How long did you take to *prepare* for this chapter?"

I'd tell you, "Oh, about thirty years!"

Most organizations are underprepared and overplanned. They say they have *strategic plans*, but in reality, they've spent their energies on the tactical issues and haven't given much thought to the broader questions and the answers that do far more to shape their future. I believe that's the easy way out. It's not difficult to *plug and play*, putting people in slots, giving assignments, allocating resources, and determining deadlines. It's much more important, though, to explore the larger issues of *what we are about* and *why we exist.* Don't take those for granted! If we get those right and the people on our leadership teams understand the significance of the *what* and the *why,* all the tactical issues will take on more meaning and people will be very motivated to accomplish them.

THREE ESSENTIAL CONCEPTS

In the past year or so, most leaders have had to dump the contents of their organizational suitcases out on the floor and start repacking! They haven't had the luxury of attending a high-level conference about the philosophy of leadership. Instead, they had to figure things out in a flash. Let me share three concepts that will help you prepare: hope for the future; rethinking the *what* and *why*; and post-pandemic planning.

1. Hope for the Future

In spite of the uncertainty you've felt during the pandemic, you've changed. You're almost certainly a better leader today than you were on January 1, 2020. You've faced shutdowns and shout-downs, craziness and critics. You've been stressed, and the strain has made you stronger. You've learned to think more strategically, love more fiercely, be present when you wanted to run and hide, and lead in the middle of adversity.

You've learned important lessons, and though none of us wants to think about it yet, we'll need those lessons when we encounter *the next normal*. Yes, that's the right term. We used to talk about a *new normal* as if it's the end point of change, but if we've learned anything in the past months, it's that change is perpetual, and we need to anticipate the next one on the horizon. It'll be a new beginning, and for church leaders, it'll be rechurch.

A crisis is like an earthquake. It shakes our confidence in our production (the what), our processes (the how), and our people (the who). You've noticed that some people in your organization have risen to meet the challenges. You may not have seen their potential before the pandemic, but somehow, the strain brought out the best in them. You see them with fresh eyes, and you're placing them in roles where they can do the most good. Leadership development may not have been on your to-do list during COVID, but there's something about being in the heat of battle together that imparts bigger leadership lessons than any other environment. But of course, you've been surprised that some people haven't exhibited the courage and creativity you hoped to see in them. The earthquake's shaking has revealed some surprising stars, but it has also exposed others who haven't contributed very much. You're different, and the people around you are different, too.

THERE'S SOMETHING ABOUT BEING IN THE HEAT OF BATTLE TOGETHER THAT IMPARTS BIGGER LEADERSHIP LESSONS THAN ANY OTHER ENVIRONMENT.

You've had to identify new ways to get things done. You were using technology before, but you quickly found ways to use it far more effectively. In this process, you streamlined your systems and structures, throwing out the old organizational chart and crafting one based on the people who have become essential to your mission.

For the rest of your career, you'll be ready for new inflection points. Hopefully, they won't be as dramatic or life-threatening as a pandemic, but scientists tell us the next one is inevitable, so we'd better be prepared. There are plenty of other inflection points that force you to think more creatively and act more courageously. Demographic shifts, racial tensions, economic turmoil, tragic disease or accidents, and other unforeseen disasters may happen gradually or in a heartbeat, but you won't be too terribly surprised by them anymore. You're ready.

2. Rethinking the *What* and the *Why*

In the middle of a crisis, we just want to survive—personally and organizationally. We instinctively triage the pressing problems to determine which ones are urgent and must be addressed now; which are beyond hope; and which can wait until tomorrow. But when the pressure subsides and we have time to reflect, we intuitively wonder what our lives are about and why we do what we do. These are the strategic questions for us as individuals and for our organizations.

THE GLUE HOLDING OUR ORGANIZATIONS TOGETHER ARE THE PEOPLE WITH THE TECHNICAL EXPERTISE TO PULL OFF THE IMPOSSIBLE IN A FEW DAYS AND THOSE WITH A WEALTH OF COMPASSION FOR OTHERS.

In "normal" times, it's easy to put our leadership on cruise control. We institute some new ideas, we fine-tune our processes, and we basically roll along from opportunity to opportunity. But a crisis shakes up our equilibrium. We desperately look for people who can come alongside us and share the load. We notice those who have technical expertise and can pull off the impossible in a few days, and we realize some of our people have a wealth of compassion for others who are suffering. They are the glue of our organizations.

The crisis has exposed what was there all along. We can't hide it any longer, and our excuses ring hollow. In an article entitled "In a Crisis, Values Matter," Richard Ades explains:

> Every crisis manifests information that provides a window into the character of a company. Transparency, integrity and decency will all shine through. Conversely, all the training and preparation money can buy cannot overcome a culture of arrogance, greed or indifference. The fact is, all crises come to an end. How companies come out the other side is largely dependent on their core values.[1]

Shaping a corporate culture isn't easy, but it's essential. The crisis has provided a golden opportunity to evaluate, ask hard questions, identify weak spots, and take steps to create an organization everyone involved can be proud of. Ades writes:

> Affecting culture takes effort, and it begins with leadership tackling reality. Companies need to dig into

their own culture and understand how a company's values inform its policies, drives the behavior of its people and clarifies purpose. A company's culture is always a work in progress. It needs constant nurturing. A company that has strong values and honest relationships with its stakeholders and customers will be more effective and resilient in a crisis, not only because of the residual good will, but because there's a clear sense of purpose.[2]

3. Post-Pandemic Planning

Now for the nuts and bolts. By the time you read this, I hope the virus is under control and businesses, schools, and churches are functioning normally...but our quick pivots during the pandemic have taught us the pros and cons of rapid change. As you consider the tactical questions of *who, how, when,* and *how much,* apply the principles you learned during the shutdowns, such as:

> » Integrate technology throughout your organization, from internal communication to marketing.

> » Elevate at least one tech wizard to your leadership team.

> » Restructure your organizational chart to reflect the new realities of your delivery systems.

> » Evaluate the flow into and out of the organization.

You may have gained some people who connected with you online, but you undoubtedly lost some, too. They may be very comfortable with staying online and away from your headquarters, store, or church, and the convenience means they've almost certainly scrolled through the sites of other businesses, churches, and nonprofits. You'll need to remind them of your value proposition so they're motivated to stay with you—or come back if they've left.

+ You'll probably have shorter meetings.

+ You'll probably have fewer meetings.

+ You'll incorporate ways to connect more meaningfully with people on your team and throughout the organization. (Compassion and authenticity are never out of style!)

ROADBLOCKS AND PITFALLS

Preparing for the future of your organization may be the last thing you want to tackle right now. I get it. The strain of leading through the pandemic has exhausted virtually every leader I know...and I know a lot of leaders! It's helpful, though, to take a long, hard look at why organizations fail in their efforts to make significant shifts in processes and products. A study by a consulting organization found that change-management efforts fail primarily in the execution phase. Leaders generally have adequate analysis and plans, and they communicate those plans fairly effectively, but when they ask people to change what they're doing (and thinking), they encountered more resistance than they expected. The study's conclusion is that the leaders were overly optimistic about the buy-in of their people. Tim Hurd, executive director of the company that conducted the survey, notes:

> Whether major or incremental, many companies are initiating changes, from transforming their business models to updating business systems and looking for ways to enhance productivity. While change is never easy for a company, it's even harder for employees.... People naturally worry what a transition will mean for them. To prevent rumors, resentment and stress, managers must quickly and continuously update staff, not just on the nuts and bolts of the change but also on how team members will be expected to contribute and, ultimately, benefit from it.[3]

The study also found that the implementation phase is only the start of a longer procedure to ingrain the new processes into the systems and people's thinking. Ongoing communication—with inspiring stories and good training—is essential for the change to take root and grow. Similarly, leadership expert Brent Gleeson identifies "1 Reason Why Most Change Management Efforts Fail." He quotes a McKinsey & Company report that 70 percent of all corporate transformations fail. There are many reasons, but one is most significant: he calls it "change battle fatigue," which he describes as "the result of many elements such as past failures plaguing the minds of employees and the sacrifices made during the arduous change process....When change efforts have failed in the past, people often grow cynical. They start to mutter under their breath, 'Here we go again...' or 'Here comes another flavor of the month...' or, as one middle manager once told me, 'We're lying low until this fad blows over.'" Gleeson is a former Navy SEAL whose brutal training has taught him a lot about resilience. He observes that the very best soldiers have been equipped mentally, physically, and relationally to endure when times are hard, but it's not always a grind. To conquer change battle fatigue, he recommends that leaders do two things: identify and celebrate early successes, which propels motivation, and create experiences that support the vision of the future, which gives people hope and tenacity.[4]

My book *New Thinking, New Future* describes the often awkward time between the leader's initial vision and its fulfillment, which I call "the muddy middle." Let me include a couple of paragraphs that certainly apply to the strains of leading during and after a crisis:

> Many leaders have observed that the hardest part of the journey to reach their dreams isn't the beginning or the end. The beginning is full of energy, hope, and enthusiasm, and the end is a great celebration, sometimes coupled with exhaustion. The middle is the problem. It's the time when enthusiasm has waned and difficulties have surfaced. People—sometimes leaders—wonder if they're on the right path, if they'll make it, and if it's worth all the trouble. A tremendous amount

of effort and money already has been expended, but the new site hasn't opened, the new product is still in development, the new software still has bugs in it, the money hasn't all been raised, and people are wondering if the leader is doing anything at all. At the beginning, everyone was motivated; at the end, there will be a party; but in the middle, skilled leaders know they continually need to inject fresh motivation because it has atrophied, and they need to celebrate each incremental step so people don't lose focus....

The ambiguous middle can be a dangerous place. If we don't pay attention, discouragement can rob us of enthusiasm, and then, apathy and confusion will creep into our leadership style and our organizations—we'll lose our cutting edge. Most failing businesses and churches begin dying about two years before there are obvious signs of decline. Like a tree with fungus in its roots, what's visible may continue to look healthy even while disease is killing it. Strong, vibrant organizations are led by people who regularly prune away dead or dying parts, fertilize often to stimulate growth, and continually add the water of vision and encouragement. They create a culture that can withstand cycles of ups and downs, expand and deepen the leadership pipeline, and introduce fresh enthusiasm through a renewed vision of the future.[5]

EMBRACING CONTINUAL PREPARATION

Some of us thrive on the challenges associated with transformational change, but most of us feel much more comfortable making only incremental changes to the way things have been. Fortunately for the first group and shockingly for the second, change is accelerating in virtually every facet of our lives. In a *Bloomberg* article on the speed of change created by technology, Barry Ritholtz observes, "We sometimes take for granted that which is right before our collective noses. Creative destruction caused by technology is so rampant that it is practically a cliche. It is easy to ignore not only the speed at which disruption caused by technology is affecting society, but the acceleration in the pace of change. This acceleration and its effect on markets, companies and labor [and every other organization] is astonishing."[6]

A buzzword that has been appearing recently in numerous articles is *agile*. Organizations with rigid systems and structures have had great difficulty pivoting quickly and effectively during the pandemic, but those that are flexible and quick have responded much better. Agile organizations can adapt to a changing environment. These companies, nonprofits, and churches have leaders who have empowered their teams to make decisions quickly, admit when they're wrong and learn from mistakes, and stay focused on the purpose through good times and bad. They have developed a culture that thrives on innovation and experiences difficulties as challenges instead of disasters.

General James Mattis has served in several top military roles, including Secretary of Defense. In a conversation with McKinsey & Company, he said that organizations need to operate "at the speed of relevance." He means that relevance is a moving target in our culture—the ways we operated only a decade ago have changed, and change isn't slowing down. Our task as leaders is to anticipate change, embrace it, instill a sense of rigorous optimism in our people, and give them room to try new things to meet the ever-changing challenges.

AGILE ORGANIZATIONS HAVE DEVELOPED A CULTURE THAT THRIVES ON INNOVATION AND EXPERIENCES DIFFICULTIES AS CHALLENGES INSTEAD OF DISASTERS.

No, we probably won't have pandemics back to back to back, but we'll face plenty of changes nonetheless. Focus on preparing yourself and your people, and watch them thrive.

TAKEAWAYS

+ Preparation is strategic; planning is tactical.

+ Most organizations are overplanned and underprepared.

+ Agile organizations are the future.

THINK ABOUT IT

1. What would I see if I looked into your organizational suitcase? In other words, what are you prepared for?

2. Does it inspire you or discourage you to be asked to rethink your *what* and *why*? Explain your answer.

3. What values has the pandemic exposed in you and your organization? How have they surfaced? Which are positive and encouraging, and which are...well, not something you hoped to see? How can you accentuate the positive and overcome the others?

4. What steps do you need to implement in your post-pandemic planning?

5. How would you describe "change battle fatigue"? How prevalent is it in your organization? How can you tell?

9

PERSONAL CARE IN CHANGING TIMES

When you face a crisis,
you know who your true friends are.
— Magic Johnson,
Hall of Fame NBA basketball player

In the early months of the pandemic, I noticed that even incredibly gifted and effective leaders were struggling. They seemed to lose focus because they were bombarded by so many changes so quickly, they seemed to lose concentration because they were mentally and physically exhausted, and they seemed to lose confidence in their ability to communicate clearly because they weren't sure what to say. For a while, I assumed these problems were directly related to organizational disruption, but as these conversations continued, I realized the source of their shaken confidence was because their families had new problems these leaders couldn't solve. They were worried about their spouse, children, grandchildren, and elderly parents.

These leaders were spending much more time at home on Zoom calls, which in some ways was very convenient, but they felt torn between the increased demands of their work and the in-your-face needs of their families. Their spouses expected them to be more attentive because they were at home; their kids often had trouble with online classes, missed their friends, and were moody; and they couldn't visit their parents, who suffered the long heartbreak of loneliness. These leaders used to be able to segment and compartmentalize their work and home life, but no longer—they had to juggle both balls all day, every day...and the balls were heavier than ever.

The demands of work multiplied. They tried very hard to maintain contact with their teams, but without casual interactions that often identified and solved problems, more things fell through the cracks. The people on their teams had the same kinds of stresses and were pulled in different directions by their family members, so everyone was on edge—with more questions and fewer readily available answers.

And people they love got sick, and some of them died. Grief was compounded because the funerals were limited to only a few people. Weddings were postponed, graduations were virtual, church doors were shut, and vacations were sporadic or cancelled.

DEEP MUSCLE BRUISES

I compare the hurt experienced by these leaders with a deep muscle bruise. Most bruises occur from bumps and cause minor bleeding just under the skin, which leaves the area *black and blue*. But a deep bruise in the thigh, calf, shoulder, upper arm, or another part of the body with substantial muscle mass may not even show on the surface, or it may have only slight discoloration—but the area is exceedingly tender and the pain is intense. Sometimes, a sprain (damage to the tendon) is associated with the muscle injury, and recovery takes even longer.

A couple of years ago, Brenda and I were in an auto accident. I would say we walked away...but that's not quite accurate. We *limped* away. Both of us had broken sternums in our chests, so every breath hurt more than we could have imagined. For a week or two, both of us felt stabbing pain in various parts of our bodies whenever we moved. Even after a month, we still hurt in some muscles, which remained very tender for a long time. As thinking, feeling beings, we have a natural aversion to pain, so in those weeks, we became cautious, moving slowly, protecting ourselves from potential injury. I think I can speak for both of us that we became somewhat obsessed with avoiding more damage to our bodies. Before the accident, we rarely thought about steering clear of a post, doorframe, or table leg, and our minds weren't consumed with what the car coming toward us might do. But pain has a way of doing two seemingly opposite things at once: distracting us and riveting our attention—distracting us from our normal desires, goals, and delights, and riveting our minds on *what ifs*, *what abouts*, and *if onlys*. The event and the pain we experienced created chronic anxiety that didn't subside until well after the healing process was over.

MANY LEADERS ARE STILL WALKING WITH A MENTAL LIMP, THEY HAVE TROUBLE SITTING IN THEIR CHAIR WITH CONFIDENT AUTHORITY, AND THEY'RE PREOCCUPIED WITH AVOIDING GETTING HURT AGAIN.

During the pandemic, leaders' souls were bruised, and many of them haven't healed yet. They're still walking with a mental limp, they have trouble sitting in their chair with confident authority, and they're preoccupied with avoiding getting hurt again. Their emotional and relational margins vanished, so they're more irritable; anxious thoughts race in their minds, their habits of eating and sleeping have changed, and they are hyperalert as they imagine the *next bad thing* that will happen. They're so self-focused that they no longer read people very well, they seldom laugh, and they're sure the divisive nature of our current cancel culture will seep into their leadership teams and tear them apart.

The health of the leader determines the health and growth of the organization. Actually, in my talks with leaders around the country and across the world, I've noticed that leaders who were healthy before the pandemic have weathered the storm fairly well. They had positive relationships with their spouse and children, they were stable financially, they handled conflict by being both direct and patient, and they enjoyed their teams. But those who weren't very healthy in one or more of these areas have been crushed under the strain. As we've seen, the crisis didn't make people healthy or unhealthy; it only revealed what already existed. During the pandemic, leaders had nowhere to hide.

LOOKING UNDER THE HOOD

It's instructive to analyze the pressures we've experienced. None of these will come as a surprise, but it's helpful to see them all together. Let's take a quick look under the hood.

MENTAL HEALTH

Symptoms of depression and anxiety have increased considerably during the pandemic. In fact, one CDC report showed that before the pandemic, 11 percent of adults reported symptoms of depression and anxiety.[1] By November 2020, that number jumped to more than 37 percent.[2] In addition, the strain of the pandemic has led to a 36 percent rise in sleep disturbance, a 32 percent increase in alcohol consumption, and a 12 percent worsening of chronic conditions.[3]

PHYSICAL HEALTH

We might think that working from home has given people more time to exercise, but that's not always the case. Two studies found a 26 to 60 percent increase is sitting, with the higher figure reflecting the impact of the pandemic on those who were most active before COVID. Sedentary behavior has increased eating and decreased the burning of calories, resulting in significant weight gain for many people[4]—some witty people say they've "gained their COVID 19"!

RELATIONAL HEALTH

Isolation—and partial isolation as we "meet" online—has disrupted how we connect with friends, family members, and coworkers, but the news isn't all bleak. Researchers at the University of Georgia launched a study, whose leader, Professor Richard Slatcher, observed: "Many people will feel very isolated, both physically and psychologically, but others may actually feel more connected to their households, neighbors and/or social networks. In fact, since launching our study, we have already heard from some people reporting that they feel more connected to others than they typically do."[5]

A partner in the study, Giulia Zoppolat from Vrije Universiteit in Amsterdam, remarked: "The way people are connecting during this time is incredibly moving—and not despite the pandemic, but because of it. We are inherently social beings, and this deep drive for connection becomes beautifully and painfully apparent in times like these."[6]

The strains of the pandemic have made people impatient with us as we lead. They may have been critics before, but now, we're afraid to look at social media to see what people are saying about us. I love the quote from Casey Stengel, the legendary manager of the New York Yankees during the glory days in the Fifties: "The secret of managing is to keep the guys who hate you away from the guys who are undecided." Great advice for all of us!

SPIRITUAL HEALTH

It's fascinating that some of the world's most respected secular organizations recognize the importance of a strong, vibrant spiritual life as leaders wrestle with the challenges of the pandemic. For instance, in a Korn Ferry article, Daniel Goleman, the author of the bestseller *Emotional Intelligence*, observes that the question "What really matters?" is "an existential query [that] has more prominence today for us all: faced with the absence of something (or in this case, many things), we become acutely aware of how important what matters to us really is. Our sense of purpose might not just be something we find ourselves mulling these days—an afterthought to our physical and mental wellbeing. There's reason to believe we would benefit from zeroing in on it."[7] An article published by the National Institutes of Health asserts that spiritual health gives people "a deeper immunity" to fight off COVID-19.[8]

The Mayo Clinic Health System offers this advice:

COVID-19 is causing many of us to think about how we are spending our time. Previously, much of our lives had been consumed by multiple activities. We are social, busy human beings by nature, so this time alone is like a new novel for all of us. One wonders if social distancing might become the new normal, so scheduling time for spiritual life-building can become part of the change of filling the void of loneliness. Concentrate on tasks and items that bring fulfillment, and increase joy and peace—particularly those that grow your spiritual life—rather than merely doing activities to fill the time.[9]

And an article posted on the website for Harvard Divinity School suggests, "In the suddenly altered pace of our lives, we might discover the stillness we all crave, the stillness from which all true wisdom and justice issue. What we love rather than what we fear may come into sharper focus—and just in time."[10]

IN THE CRUSH OF HAVING TO MAKE SNAP DECISIONS— AND EXPERIENCING BOTH INTERNAL DOUBTS AND EXTERNAL PUSHBACK—IT'S IMPORTANT TO STAY CLOSELY CONNECTED TO THE ONLY TRUE SOURCE OF STABILITY, WISDOM, AND JOY.

In the crush of having to make snap decisions—and experiencing both internal doubts and external pushback—it's important to stay closely connected to the only true source of stability, wisdom, and joy.

FINANCIAL HEALTH

At this writing, the rich have gotten much richer during the pandemic, but income disparity has grown. Those who were already doing well are watching their portfolios swell, but millions of others are straining to put food on the table for their families. Even if you're in the first category, you have at least some connections with people on the other end of the spectrum. For those who are trying to make it through this rough time of unemployment and sustained expenses, budgeting is especially important. For all of us, our generosity makes a visible and tangible difference in the lives of people who are struggling. And leaders may be worried about how all the disruption of the pandemic is affecting—and will continue to affect—their employees, their processes and systems, and their bottom line.

The question, then, is how can leaders rebuild margin and restore health to every aspect of their lives? I'm glad you asked.

FIND A FRIEND

We're wounded in relationships, and we're healed in relationships. God has made us so that we only function well when we give and receive love. We need at least one person who doesn't run away or laugh when we share our deepest secrets, who listens intently, speaks wisdom and grace, keeps confidences, and accepts us as we are, not as we should be. Do you have someone like that?

Good listeners have a powerful impact on others. I recall that when I was a pastor and people came to talk to me about a problem, they often talked for fifty-five minutes during the hour we had together. I nodded, uttered "Uh huh" a few times, and occasionally said, "I'm so sorry that happened," or "Tell me more about that." At the end of our time, I had given virtually no input, no sweeping analysis, and no treasures of wisdom, but they often walked out saying, "That was so helpful! Thank you so much. Can I come back next week?"

The leaders of ancient Israel and Judah identified six towns as "cities of refuge," where people who had accidentally killed someone could go for asylum. These were safe places for people on the run.

Who are the people who give you *a safe space to be yourself*?

During the pandemic, when many churches saw contributions decline, I received an email from a pastor. It read, "Sam, an amazing thing happened today. A lady walked into my office and handed me a check for $100,000. I don't think she had any idea how much our church needs this money. I want to shout my thanks from the roof of the church, but I'm afraid a lot of other pastors in our area wouldn't appreciate us receiving a substantial gift...one they didn't get. Sam, you're the only person I can tell about this wonderful news."

The Bible tells us, *"Rejoice with those who rejoice, weep with those who weep"* (Romans 12:15). I've discovered a strange paradox that there are multitudes of people who will weep with us, but we can count those who will truly rejoice with us on one hand. Think of it this way: if a rich relative died and left you $50 million, who would you tell? You probably wouldn't feel comfortable telling everyone you know because they might respond by seeking a handout...or with a grimace that says, "Why you and not me?" But on the other hand, if you were in a car accident and broke your leg, you'd post pictures on social media and let everyone know what happened. If your house caught on fire, you'd send a text, email, or post to let people know...and maybe give you a place to stay for a week or two.

This isn't just theory to me. When Brenda and I paid off the mortgage on our house a few years ago, we were really excited, but we instantly realized that the only people who could fully enjoy it with us were our daughters, Rachel and Debbie. To us, it was a celebration, but others might have seen our joy as bragging, or they might have assumed we were tone-deaf to those who are financially challenged.

As leaders, we need a friend or two who aren't jealous or threatened by our deepest joys, and there are far fewer of them than people who will share our heartaches. If we believe we're completely safe with someone, we'll feel invited to share our full range of hopes and fears, triumphs and tragedies, blessings and struggles.

BENCHMARKS

Let's look at some diagnostic questions that help us measure the quality of our friendships.

ARE YOUR MOST IMPORTANT RELATIONSHIPS TRANSACTIONAL?

Some leaders have been promoted to their positions because they proved they can build strong relationships on their teams and encourage them to give their best, but others are classic Type A personalities: driven, tenacious, and demanding. I've known some leaders whose connections with people, even people in their own families, were entirely transactional. They were in it only for themselves, and each person was valuable only if they contributed to the leader's accomplishments. Of course, transactional relationships are perfectly fine when you buy groceries, fill up your car with gas, and pick up the laundry. We might engage in some superficial pleasantries, but we're connecting with these people primarily for our individual benefit. There's nothing wrong with that.

But there's something terribly wrong if selfishness is the primary factor in our most important relationships. When this happens, people feel used because they *are* being used! Connections to family and friends are more than business deals; they're meant to be sources of comfort, understanding, validation, and joy—but many aren't. Some relationships at home and at work are little more than an armed truce; both sides are waiting for the other to fire a shot, and the war will quickly escalate again. When we're transactional in our important relationships, we want to win in every conflict or disagreement; when we're relational, we work hard to resolve conflict so both sides feel understood, affirmed, and appreciated.

WHAT ARE THE QUALITIES OF TRUE FRIENDSHIP?

Author and pastor Tim Keller outlines four marks of a genuine friend: constancy, carefulness, candor, and counsel. Constancy means the person is a friend in all circumstances: the great, the terrible, and everything in between. Carefulness is when a friend holds your heart tenderly in his hands, cherishing it and knowing that it might break. Candor isn't just being blunt; it's a beautiful blend of grace and truth, knowing that sometimes honest words hurt, but only like a surgeon's scalpel hurts as it heals. And counsel is the wisdom and will to give advice, but only if it's requested, knowing the person so well that we understand how to say it so he can receive it.[11] This blend of qualities is rare for a number of reasons: we're distracted and busy; we're mobile so we don't put down roots; we don't want to invest the necessary time; and we see people like this as...well, kind of strange.

DO YOU HAVE ANY REAL FRIENDS?

In our organizations, we often feel isolated. We're leaders, and our people are followers. They don't understand the pressures we feel, and they don't wrestle with the complexities that rumble through our minds day and night. We've arrived at a position of authority, and they—at least some of them—are jockeying for the next rung up the ladder, so we're a bit suspicious of their desire to be friends. Some of us have been burned in the past, and we won't let our guard down now. Holding them at a distance seems perfectly reasonable and appropriate.

BUT HERE'S THE TRUTH: IF YOU DON'T HAVE FRIENDS, YOU'RE ON THE ROAD TO BURNOUT. WRITE IT DOWN—I GUARANTEE IT.

But here's the truth: if you don't have friends, you're on the road to burnout. Write it down—I guarantee it. God has made us relational creatures, and we need love and understanding like a fish needs water. We may be able to toughen up and go on for several years, but sooner or later, we'll crater.

My recommendation isn't to make your team members your best friends. They may be somewhere in your sphere of friendships, but it's much better to find a peer or two outside the organization. You may become close to someone who is in the same field as you, or someone who is in a completely different line of work. The point is that you're not depending on each other for professional advancement, so you're not competing with each other. When you get together, you can be totally transparent without fear that your friend will use your honesty against you.

In times of crisis and loss, people often become more transparent and reveal more of their hearts. When the pandemic entered its second surge in the summer of 2020, a leader on the West Coast called to talk with me. In my work as a consultant, I field a lot of very specific leadership questions, but early in this conversation, I realized this call was different. I asked him, "Tell me how you're doing? How's your family coping with all the uncertainty?"

After a few seconds, he told me, "Sam, my mother died, but I wasn't allowed to be with her. She had been in the ICU for two weeks. I've seen that happening in the news reports, but I never imagined it would happen to us." He then explained that his two children had struggled with online school, missed their friends, and were bored at home—all of which caused them to be more irritable, which created more tension for him and his wife. All of this was plenty to wrestle with, but the family disruption was in addition to the loss of his mother and the myriad of organizational struggles at work.

"Is there anyone there you can have coffee with?" I suggested. "Anyone who is a real friend?"

"That's why I'm calling you, Sam. That's why I'm calling you."

During the pandemic, we've discovered our true friends. In the rush of trying to take care of business, we may not talk regularly, but when we do, we pick up right where we left off. The power of friendships has an immediate and a lasting effect. In the moment when we understand and feel understood, we get a rush of brain chemicals that tell us things are going to be all right. And days and weeks later, we have a bedrock confidence that no matter what happens, there's someone we can count on...and that means the world to us.

In this chapter, I have not given you "ten tips to have a balanced life." Our lives have been anything but balanced during COVID! But even when life is chaotic, having a true friend or two brings stability, hope, understanding, and a sense that someone cares with no strings attached. Cultivating these relationships is our first priority in personal care.

TAKEAWAYS

+ Leaders have suffered deep muscle bruises during the pandemic, and the pain lingers.

+ We need at least a friend or two as "cities of refuge."

+ Cultivating real friendships takes time and energy, but it's well worth it.

THINK ABOUT IT

1. What are some of the ways leading during the pandemic has inflicted "deep muscle bruises" in your soul?

2. If a very perceptive person could observe you for a week, how would they evaluate your mental, relational, spiritual, and financial health?

3. Do you agree or disagree that the most important factor in personal care is cultivating one or two authentic friendships? Explain your answer.

4. How would you amplify the descriptions of the four qualities of friendship: constancy, carefulness, candor, and counsel?

5. What specific steps will you take to find this kind of friend or cultivate the ones you have?

ABOUT THE AUTHOR

Sam Chand's singular vision for his life is to help others succeed. A prolific author and renowned international business consultant, he develops leaders through consultations, the Sam Chand Leadership Institute, Dream Releaser Coaching, *AVAIL Journal*, Inspire Collective, and other resources such as books, webinars, and digital downloads.

Sam consults with large churches, nonprofits, and businesses on leadership and growth, conducts worldwide leadership conferences, and speaks regularly at corporations, business roundtables, seminars, and other leadership development opportunities.

Being raised in a pastor's home in India has uniquely equipped Sam to share his passion to mentor, develop, and inspire leaders to break all limits. He has been called a dream releaser, leadership architect, and change strategist.

In the 1970s, as a student at Beulah Heights Bible College, Sam served as a janitor, cook, and dishwasher to finance his education. He returned in 1989 as president—and under his leadership, Beulah Heights University became the country's largest predominantly African-American Christian college.

Sam holds an honorary Doctor of Humane Letters from Beulah Heights University, an honorary Doctor of Divinity from Heritage Bible College, a Master of Arts in Biblical Counseling from Grace Theological Seminary, and a Bachelor of Arts in Biblical Education from Beulah Heights. He has mentored leaders in churches and ministries as well as international corporations and business start-ups. He was named one of the top thirty global leadership gurus by www.leadershipgurus.net.

Sam has authored more than twenty books on leadership, including *Harnessing the Power of Tension: Stretched but Not Broken*; *The Sequence to Success: Three O's That Will Take You Anywhere in Life*; *New Thinking, New Future*; *Culture Catalyst*; *Bigger Faster Leadership*; *Who's Holding Your Ladder?*; and *Leadership Pain*.

Sam and his wife Brenda have two adult daughters. They make their home in Atlanta, Georgia.

For more information or to connect with Sam, please visit www.samchand.com.

ENDNOTES

CHAPTER 1: NEVER THE SAME AGAIN

1. Laura Spinney, "The World Changed Its Approach to Health After the 1918 Flu. Will It After the COVID-19 Outbreak?", *TIME*, March 7, 2020 (time.com/5797629/health-1918-flu-epidemic).

2. Anne Sraders and Lance Lambert, "Nearly 100,000 establishments that temporarily shut down due to the pandemic are now out of business," *Fortune*, September 28, 2020 (fortune.com/2020/09/28/covid-buisnesses-shut-down-closed).

3. Michael Brendan Dougherty, "The Sick Year," *National Review*, February 10, 2021 (www.nationalreview.com/2021/02/the-sick-year).

4. "COVID-19 and multiorgan failure," National Institutes of Health (www.ncbi.nlm.nih.gov/pmc/articles/PMC7533045/#:~:text=COVID%2D19%20also%20is,al.%202020).

5. Julianne Holt-Lunstad, "The Double Pandemic Of Social Isolation And COVID-19: Cross-Sector Policy Must Address Both," *Health Affairs*, June 22, 2020 (www.healthaffairs.org/do/10.1377/hblog20200609.53823).

6. "Reimagining the postpandemic organization," *McKinsey Quarterly*, May 15, 2020 (www.mckinsey.com/business-functions/organization/our-insights/reimagining-the-post-pandemic-organization).

7. "The Shortlist," McKinsey & Company, August 7, 2020 (www.mckinsey.com/~/media/McKinsey/Email/Shortlist/99/2020-08-7.html).

CHAPTER 2: THREE MASSIVE SHIFTS

1. Falon Fatemi, "3 Ways Covid-19 Will Permanently Change the Future of Work," *Forbes*, June 3, 2020 (www.forbes.com/sites/falonfatemi/2020/06/03/3-ways-covid-19-will-permanently-change-the-future-of-work/?sh=5604412065b1).

2. Michael Jacobides and Martin Reeves, "Adapt Your Business to the New Reality," *Harvard Business Review*, September-October 2020 (hbr.org/2020/09/adapt-your-business-to-the-new-reality).

3. Jennifer Clopton, "COVID Stressing the Nation's Stress Therapy System," *WebMD*, January 8, 2021 (www.webmd.com/lung/news/20210108/covid-stressing-the-nations-stress-therapy-system).

4. Ibid.

5. Rita McGrath, "Thoughts in the Midst of an Inflection Point," Rita McGrath Group, March 20, 2020 (www.ritamcgrath.com/2020/03/thoughts-in-the-midst-of-an-inflection-point).

CHAPTER 3: THE PACE OF CHANGE

1. Rhett Power, "How 5 Businesses Are Adapting to Life in a Pandemic," *Forbes*, April 26, 2020 (www.forbes.com/sites/rhettpower/2020/04/26/how-5-businesses-are-adapting-to-life-in-a-pandemic/?sh=169996d44f5a).

2. Dana Rubinstein, Juliana Kim, Troy Closson and Michael Gold, "As New York City's Covid-19 Lockdown Nears, Confusion and Anger Reign," *The New York Times*, October 20, 2020, (www.nytimes.com/live/2020/10/08/world/covid-coronavirus).

CHAPTER 4: PEOPLE OF CHANGE

1. *Change Management Leadership Guide*, Ryerson University Human Resources, 2011, p. 11.

2. Krister Ungerböck, "Why introvert leaders excel during a crisis," *Fast Company*, May 12, 2020, (www.fastcompany.com/90503743/why-introverted-leaders-excel-during-a-crisis).

3. Megan L. Evans, M.D., M.P.H., Margo Lindauer, J.D., and Maureen E. Farrell, M.D., "A Pandemic within a Pandemic—Intimate Partner Violence during Covid-19," *The New England Journal of Medicine*, December 2020, (www.nejm.org/doi/full/10.1056/NEJMp2024046).

4. Kristopher T. Kang, MD, and Nita Jain, MD, FRCPC, "Child Abuse and Neglect in the COVID-19 Era: A Primer for Front-Line Physicians in British Columbia," *BC Medical Journal*, September 2020 (bcmj.org/articles/child-abuse-and-neglect-covid-19-era-primer-front-line-physicians-british-columbia).

5. Emilio Marrero, "Survey: Alcohol and Drug Use Increase During Covid-19 Pandemic," Baptist Health South Florida, September 10, 2020 (baptisthealth.net/baptist-health-news/alcohol-and-drug-use-on-the-rise-during-covid-19-pandemic).

6. Sarah Schwartz, "Survey: Teachers and Students Are Struggling with Online Learning," *Education Week*, November 16, 2020 (www.edweek.org/teaching-learning/survey-teachers-and-students-are-struggling-with-online-learning/2020/11).

7. Charles Stone, "8 Neurological Reasons Why Church Change Is So Difficult," *Outreach Magazine*, March 5, 2018 (outreachmagazine.com/features/leadership/27000-8-neurological-reasons-church-change-difficult.html).

8. Kim Pope, "Why Empathy Is Vital for Effective Leadership, Especially in Times of Crisis," *Forbes*, June 19, 2020 (www.forbes.com/sites/forbeshumanresourcescouncil/2020/06/19/why-empathy-is-vital-for-effective-leadership-especially-in-times-of-crisis/?sh=4a81633d449f).

9. Carolyn Dewar, Scott Keller, Kevin Sneader, and Kurt Strovink, "The CEO moment: Leadership for a new era," *McKinsey Quarterly*, July 21, 2020 (www.mckinsey.com/featured-insights/leadership/the-ceo-moment-leadership-for-a-new-era).

CHAPTER 5: THE PROCESS OF CHANGE

1. Dr. Tim Elmore, "Inseparable: The Sobering Truth About Tomorrow's Leaders," *Growing Leaders*, September 10, 2013 (growingleaders.com/blog/inseparable-sobering-truth-tomorrows-leaders).

2. Charles Conn and Robert McLean, "Six problem-solving mindsets for very uncertain times," *McKinsey Quarterly*, September 15, 2020 (www.mckinsey.com/business-functions/strategy-and-corporate-finance/our-insights/six-problem-solving-mindsets-for-very-uncertain-times).

3. Ibid. For more from Chris Bradley, in a conversation with Rob McLean, see "Want better strategies? Become a bulletproof problem solver," McKinsey & Company, August 8, 2019 (www.mckinsey.com/business-functions/strategy-and-corporate-finance/our-insights/want-better-strategies-become-a-bulletproof-problem-solver).

4. Melissa Swift, "Choose Your Own Future," Korn Ferry (focus.kornferry.com/wp-content/uploads/2015/02/Korn-Ferry-Choose-your-own-future.pdf).

CHAPTER 6: PROGRAMS IN CHANGE

1. Jon Wertheim, "Companies and Foreign Countries Vying for Your DNA," *60 Minutes*, January 31, 2021, (www.cbsnews.com/news/dna-genealogy-privacy-60-minutes-2021-01-31).

2. "Forcing Change: Driving Innovation and Delivering Results," Brett Ridge and Brian Reich, CDS Global, 2013.

3. From *Leading Change* by John Kotter, adapted by *Leadership Wired*, Issue 1.

4. Gary Burnison, "It's Time to Be Vulnerable," Korn Ferry, May 10, 2020 (www.kornferry.com/insights/special-edition/vulnerability-leadership-coronavirus).

5. Ibid.

CHAPTER 7: PROCLAMATION IN CHANGE

1. Scott Pelley, "Stories from those who lost loved ones to COVID-19," *60 Minutes*, January 31, 2021 (www.cbsnews.com/news/covid-19-deaths-families-60-minutes-2021-01-31).

CHAPTER 8: PREPARATION FOR CHANGE

1. Richard Ades, "In a Crisis, Values Matter," *Corporate Board Member* (boardmember.com/crisis-values-matter).

2. Ibid.

3. "Where Change Management Fails," Robert Half Management Resources, February 3, 2016 (rh-us.mediaroom.com/2016-02-03-Where-Change-Management-Fails).

4. Brent Gleeson, "1 Reason Why Most Change Management Efforts Fail," *Forbes*, July 25, 2017 (www.forbes.com/sites/brentgleeson/2017/07/25/1-reason-why-most-change-management-efforts-fail/?sh=f413194546b7).

5. Samuel R. Chand, *New Thinking, New Future* (New Kensington, PA: Whitaker House, 2019), 36–37.

6. Barry Ritholtz, "The World Is About to Change Even Faster," *Bloomberg*, July 6, 2017 (www.bloomberg.com/opinion/articles/2017-07-06/the-world-is-about-to-change-even-faster).

CHAPTER 9: PERSONAL CARE IN CHANGING TIMES

1. "Early Release of Selected Mental Health Estimates Based on Data from the January–June 2019 National Health Interview Survey" (www.cdc.gov/nchs/data/nhis/earlyrelease/ERmentalhealth-508.pdf).

2. "Anxiety and Depression Household Pulse Survey" (www.cdc.gov/nchs/covid19/pulse/mental-health.htm).

3. Nirmita Panchal, Rabah Kamal, Cynthia Cox, and Rachel Garfield, "The Implications of COVID-19 for Mental Health and Substance Abuse," KFF, February 10, 2021 (www.kff.org/coronavirus-covid-19/issue-brief/the-implications-of-covid-19-for-mental-health-and-substance-use).

4. Jacob E. Barkley, et al., "The Acute Effects of the COVID-19 Pandemic on Physical Activity and Sedentary Behavior in University Students and Employees," National Institutes of Health, September 1, 2020 (www.ncbi.nlm.nih.gov/pmc/articles/PMC7523895).

5. Tyler Wilkins, "Researchers study COVID's effect on relationships," UGA Today, April 8, 2020 (news.uga.edu/research-covid19-effect-on-relationships).

6. Ibid.

7. Daniel Goleman, "'Spiritual' Health in the Pandemic," Korn Ferry, (www.kornferry.com/insights/articles/spiritual-health-purpose-coronavirus).

8. Nicolette V. Roman, Thuli G. Mthembu, and Mujeeb Hoosen, "Spiritual care—'A deeper immunity—A response to Covid-19 pandemic," NIH, June 15, 2020 (www.ncbi.nlm.nih.gov/pmc/articles/PMC7343955).

9. William Creech, "Building your spiritual life during changes brought about by the COVID-19 pandemic," Mayo Clinic Health System (www.mayoclinichealthsystem.org/hometown-health/speaking-of-health/building-your-spiritual-life-during-covid-19-changes).

10. Kerry Maloney, "Spiritual Resources During the COVID Pandemic," Harvard Divinity School, (hds.harvard.edu/life-at-hds/religious-and-spiritual-life/spiritual-resources-during-covid-19-pandemic).

11. Adapted from "Friendship," Tim Keller, December 18, 2015 (reformedevangelist.blogspot.com/2015/12/a-transcription-of-tim-kellers_18.html).

RECEIVE **FREE LEADERSHIP TRAINING** IN YOUR INBOX EVERY TUESDAY!

In these videos, I share a 2-3 minute nugget that will enhance your leadership.

Sign up for free! www.samchand.com

OTHER BOOKS BY SAM CHAND

NEW THINKING, NEW FUTURE

The way leaders think matters—it matters a lot. The problem is that we almost universally make a colossal subconscious assumption that the way we think is the only possible way to consider our situations...We need to upgrade the software in our heads!

CULTURE CATALYST

Often, organizational leaders confuse culture with vision and strategy, but they are very different. Vision and strategy usually focus on products, services, and outcomes, but culture is about the people—an organization's most valuable asset.

BIGGER, FASTER LEADERSHIP

More passion isn't the answer, and bigger dreams aren't always the solution. Every leader is asking two questions: How can we grow? How can we grow faster? The only way organizations can grow bigger and move faster is by accelerating the excellence of their systems and structures.

LEADERSHIP PAIN

Do you want to be a better leader? Raise the threshold of your pain. Do you want your church to grow or your business to reach higher goals? Reluctance to face pain is your greatest limitation. There is no growth without change, no change without loss, and no loss without pain.

AVAILABLE ON AMAZON OR ANYWHERE BOOKS ARE SOLD

GET FREE ACCESS TO MODULE ONE
OF THE *SAM CHAND LEADERSHIP INSTITUTE!*

The **Sam Chand Leadership Institute** is a virtual environment where high-performing leaders gather to create success, grow their network, and expand their capacity for more.

SAMCHANDLEADERSHIP.COM/SPECIAL

Welcome to Our House!

We Have a Special Gift for You

It is our privilege and pleasure to share in your love of Christian books. We are committed to bringing you authors and books that feed, challenge, and enrich your faith.

To show our appreciation, we invite you to sign up to receive a specially selected **Reader Appreciation Gift**, with our compliments. Just go to the Web address at the bottom of this page.

God bless you as you seek a deeper walk with Him!

WE HAVE A GIFT FOR YOU. VISIT:

whpub.me/nonfictionthx

WHITAKER
HOUSE